T0375704

Engine 49
Devil's Night

Engine 49
Devil's Night

Duane Hollywood Abrams
SUPERFIREMAN

iUniverse, Inc.
Bloomington

Engine 49 Devil's Night
Superfireman

Note to the reader: Many of the names have been changed to keep their identities private, also many of the fire stories, and love life experiences, may not be in their proper timeline, to create an entertaining, yet understandable story.

Fire photos by Bill Eisner

billeinser/Photo1Detroit.sumgmug.com

Front cover and back by Pedro

iUniverse books may be ordered through booksellers or by contacting:

iUniverse
1663 Liberty Drive
Bloomington, IN 47403
www.iuniverse.com
1-800-Authors (1-800-288-4677)

ISBN: 978-1-4620-5913-3 (sc)
ISBN: 978-1-4620-5914-0 (e)

Printed in the United States of America

iUniverse rev. date: 03/09/2012

Table of Contents

Chapter 1
THE BLAZE

A TALL MAN IN DARK clothing walked into the loading bay of the Mac-o-lac paint factory. He looked like a truck driver wearing a dark cap and sunglasses, he walked toward the restroom with a box, smoking a cigarette. When he walked out of the restroom his hands were full of paper towel as he dried them off. Then the stranger walked out the plant to the parking lot, he lit another cigarette walking to his truck. Everyone was working and no one paid him any attention he walked in and out without notice. It was just another day of work on a beautiful sunny morning.

In a paint factory or any company that uses or stores flammable liquids, fire is the enemy that they are always on guard for, always on the watch to prevent any accidents that could create a fire. A pile of rags or a mattress can burn slowly for hours without any notice of flames, just smoke. An uncaring smoker tosses a cigarette in a trash

1

can and it smolders. The smoke is so faint that no one notices. Slowly it grows while everyone is busy doing their jobs. The fire finally ignites burning paper and rags in a garbage can. The fire grows quickly as it dances high enough to catch a box on a shelf, then goes to the ceiling. The man walks past the guards and out the door, once past the bay doors and to his truck. He opened the door to his truck and gets in, as soon as the door shut, there was a explosion in the factory. When fire burns it searches for fuel in any and every direction, and when it finds it, Boom . . . . Boom . . . . Boom . . . . Boom. He looked out the window calmly while starting up the truck, puffed on his cigarette and pulled out of the lot. In the Mac-o-lac paint factory was a series of explosions, which caught everyone off guard, Boom . . . . Boom . . . . Boom . . . . Boom. The guard in the parking lot called 911, the explosion set off the fire alarm, while many workers called 911 as they ran out of the factory. Workers dressed in white lab coats ran to the door. One worker fell while running and another helped him up as they ran to the emergency exit. In the office the alarm was ringing as an official wearing a suit and tie grabbed some papers and stuffed them in a briefcase then quickly walked out his office. The other workers in the office were startled he told them "there is a fire in the factory everyone out, don't run!" The ladies got their purses and quickly went to the door. There was a large crowd in the front of the office as they all went outside, talking as they got outside. Boom . . . . . . .Boom . . . . .Boom . . . . .Boom. Red lights were flashing, the alarm was blasting loudly, the factory workers evacuated crowding the stairways as they all poured outside.

Grand Central was where all the calls came in, the board lit up with lights all surrounding the address 12345 Schaefer, the Mac-o-lac paint factory. The computer shot out all the information on the factory, which is over a million gallons of flammable liquids on their property and in a silo on the outside. "Send Engine 49, 53, 30, Ladder company 21, Squad 5, and Chief 4 to check it out" said one dispatch in the radio microphone. Meanwhile back at the factory was chaos Boom . . . . Boom . . . .

Boom . . . . Boom . . . . a living hell. The fire leaped out the big bay doors, like a dragon. The deafening booms filled the air like the cannons from the civil war. The fire rose fifty to a hundred feet in the sky as the explosions beat like the 808 low bass drum in a House Music tune. The man in the truck with dark sun glasses on made a call while driving away. "It's done" then he closed his phone and sped away, hitting the I-96 expressway.

Arsonist : a person that is secretly given information, resources, and a payment to burn a building, car, or area, for purposes of collecting insurance, getting rid of a burden, clear an area, or just having fun.

Pyromaniac : a person that enjoys setting and watching fires.

Frustration and anger can trigger a desire to burn something that will release the tension.

Sometimes little boys and girls are fascinated with fire so much they play with matches or a lighter.

After White flight in the sixties and seventies over one million homes, and businesses in Detroit have burned by arsonists with damages costing Billions of dollars.

All it takes is a match or a cigarette, thrown in the wrong place, on some paper or greasy rags, and it can produce a roaring blaze. It will start small, an ember glowing orange, growing all the time breathing consuming anything flammable in its path.

Fire or Combustion is a living breathing creature, capable of destroying whole cities at a time.

The stars in the sky are whole planets on fire. In the ancient years of long ago fire was a God.

It's not the fire that kills, it's Carbon Monoxide an invisible tasteless odorless fume that is created from combustion that kills in minutes. The way it kills is by seduction, it slowly enters the nostrils going straight to the brain like a snake putting you into a deeper sleep like a hypnotic trance.

Smoke to the brain is a death sentence, silent tranquil sleep.

Smoke is the first trace of combustion, a smell of burning.

Without oxygen a fire will burn slow and eventually go out, but when given enough oxygen, fuel, from a spark you've got a fire.

There only three ways to stop a fire:

1) To stop the oxygen and smother it

2) To take away the fuel, or anything flammable in its way

3) To expose it to water from a lake, or a hose powered from a underground water supply, in which I'm an expert at, using my hose and pipe to throw water on it, till it goes out!

Engine house 49, Grand River at Manor in the City of Detroit 1027 hours]

The cook is out shopping for the day, and we just got finished cleaning up the station. The engineer checked out the Mack pumper, and I was making soup out of the leftovers from yesterday. The soup was almost ready when an alarm came across on the Box alert system. There was aloud ringing bell went off the lights came on, as the ticker tape clicked off 4-7-2. A skinny young man shouted "this is our box we're first, it's right around the corner down Fullerton". That was Freddie the fire buff that lived around the corner, always at the station doing something. I yelled "we got a Box" then I dropped everything, ran back in the kitchen and turned off the soup. I ran to the apparatus room put on my boots and jumped on the engine. The old Mack Pumper started up kicking out exhaust all over the room. Grey and black smoke filled the air as we roared out. The big red doors opened as we flew out on Grand River, spilling water everywhere we went. One quick left then at the light we hit Fullerton with our sirens blaring, air horn honking. I could see the dark clouds forming in the air, as we sped to Schaefer Avenue. In the sky I saw the flame dancing fifty feet in the air. I pulled my coat over my shoulders, and slipped my arms in the harness of my oxygen tank. I dropped my air mask over my head and I buckled it up on my chest. I reached my hand behind me as I turned on the tank, a small bell went off. I looked at my register to see how much air was in the tank it was full. We got closer as I put my mask on my neck, put my helmet on and grabbed my axe. When we hit Schaefer we made a left, then a right into the parking lot. I saw the address pass over my head (12345) as we drove through the gates. We headed for the mouth of the dragon, as it spit, fireball after fireball as booming noises would explode with each burst. Boom . . . . Boom . . . . Boom . . . . Boom.

I looked ahead as we sped to the back, through an asphalt rocky driveway, kicking the rocks back and forth. Lt Maher was in charge today, he was one of my favorite bosses. Lt Maher was a thin medium height older white gentleman, with nerves of steel. He knew the job and knew it well, he was an expert fire fighter, and working under him was a pleasure. The Fire Engine Operator McPhail could have been a sharp southern moonshine driver the way he hit the streets, his speed and accuracy racing through the Kentucky Hills back roads escaping the sheriff. FEO McPhail was a very dedicated Engineer, he would completely check out the whole rig everyday to make sure everything was working properly. Senior Fire Fighter Kalusney was out shopping for the day, and I was riding the back end, Pipeman Fire Fighter Abrams a nineteen years old street kid from Detroit.

This was a nice warm summer day and on it's way to being the longest day in DETROIT fire fighting history. A large Paint Factory around the corner about a quarter of a mile from the engine house. Maybe it was a careless smoker or a spark, whatever happen is now a raging inferno at this two story high brick factory half a city block long. The fire was blazing out the port bay doors, every couple of seconds another explosive burst of flames would roll out. Boom . . . . Boom . . . . Boom . . . . Boom. The fire started in the loading dock where there were several fifty-gallon drums of paint, and other flammable chemicals being transported by trucks. As the heat from the flames would ignite each drum one by one, as they erupted with a deafening roar. BOOM, BOOM, BOOM, BOOM, BOOM, BOOM. The fire would roll out the mouth of the bay doors, one after another, at an unceasing rapid pace. I was scared, and excited at the same time, I was all jumpy on the inside all I could do was look eyes bucked wide open as we pulled closer. We were the first to arrive, Engine 30, Ladder 21, Engine 53, and Squad 5 were about 5 to 10 minutes behind us. Lt Maher got on the Radio and called this in as a four Alarm Fire.

Now this is a four alarm fire, they will send three more Engine companies, two more ladder companies, a Squad, and a Senior Chief. Lt. Maher shouted grab the 2 ½ and dump both beds. The Engine turned around and backed up as close as we could get to the fire. When he stopped I jumped off the back end, and threw all the hoses to the ground, as FEO McPhail took off for the hydrant. All the lines started flying in the air like spaghetti, as he pulled up on the Hydrant about a hundred feet away. Lt Maher and I stood there with the limp line at our feet. I unraveled the hose and got 2 ½ foot Akron pipe. We were so close that we could see waves of a shimmering curtain of intense heat right in front of us. Then we set up the line by pulling out the two 2 ½ foot Akron pipes, and untangled the hose. We set up two spots aimed at the bay doors and waited for water. Each line had a seventy-five pound Akron nozzle connected to them, which needs at lease two to three men to hold them after they are charged. Lt Maher and

I were on the first line, then another company showed up Engine 30, and they got on the second line. We just stood there with our clothes smoking from the heat as we looked upon the fire. I saw a friend of mine from the academy, he was jumping around very nervously. He said, "if this place goes up it will take a ten block radius with it, I'm out of here man". Then he ran off into the crowd of fire fighters coming on the scene. The fire just roared on blasting, fireball after fireball, explosion after explosion with deafening BOOMS! We just waited there for the water with our mouths wide open. Looking at the line laid down the driveway, past the street, on the other side, at the hydrant. FEO McPhail was not only the fastest driver, but he was also one of the quickest hook-up Engineers on the department. WATER, WATER, WATER !!! "You've got water" is what they yelled, one after another. We looked at the line as they started to fill with water. They looked like snakes flipping around as the lines swelled in size. Lt Maher got a transmission off the radio, orders from the chief. Then he told us to make a water shield between the loading dock and the storage tower. The storage tower is filled with flammable chemicals. If ignited or heated it could blow up everything in a 10 mile squared radius. We were given the orders to charge the lines, by Lt. Maher. When I opened my line a mist of water came out first, then the water sprayed out like a hydrant on a hot day. There were three of us on one line. Because I was the youngest I was at the front end. One man was on the back of the line about three feet away from the two on the pipe. The pipe is like a big gun, two feet long, chrome plated, with shut off in the middle, the pipeman is at the front by the nozzle and the other fire fighter right behind him is his back-up. I held the nozzle in position, not at the fire but between the loading bay and the flammable silo. This was different because Detroit Fire fighters are trained to attack a fire, by running straight in and putting the fire out from the inside. Because of the explosions, and the flammable liquid, it would be too dangerous to go inside. If we put the water on the fire it might push it in the direction of the flammable storage tower.

We used our lines to make a water blanket, and everyone else fought the fire from other sides. As I shot the water in between the fire and the silo, I starred at the mouth of the fire raging out the bay doors. Every time a barrel would explode, I would jump, thinking that was the one that would blow us all up. That day barrel after barrel exploded, fireball after fireball would roll out getting closer and closer to the silo. All I could think of was this would be my last day on earth. Now I would find out if God really exist.

The other fire fighters worked on the fire. They set up water towers (that is when a 2 ½ inch line with a special nozzle is put on a 200 foot ladder truck extended in the air over the building) and began to dump water on the building. Because of the danger we all stayed back as far as we could to still be effective. The ladder companies set their towers up and the engine companies got ready the to attack the building. Since we were the first engine and committed to the water shield we had to stay there and pour hundreds of gallons of water, in between the storage silo for hours. It always seems as though it would never go out, but all we could do was shoot gallons after gallons, hour after hour. Fire fighters were running around doing all kinds of fire maneuvers, laying line, putting up ladders, and trying to set up to put the fire out. My mind drifted off after hours of sitting on the ground with the Akron two and a half foot pipe in my lap, pumping water on this working fire.

I have always been in training for as long as I can remember. Running, push-ups, sit-ups, climbing, jumping, lifting weights, throwing, from sun up till sun set. If I had stuck to Sergeant Rod's plan I would be much stronger now. The Sergeant believed that we should work-out till it hurts, then work thru the pain. No Pain No Gain. After the pain is where the power is, this is the realm of Greatness.

While growing up I wanted to become first a fullback on any professional football team. Then I was considering entering the field of science, maybe an astronaut, or a USAir Force Pilot. This is what I really wanted. Now that I'm a fire fighter I know that all my training has paid off. My earliest memories of growing up in a three bedroom brick house on the north west side of the city. I knew that one day I would do something great. I knew

I was being built for something special. In our home we studied to become supermen. When there was not a car in the drive way it was my oldest brother Staff Sergeant Rod head of the household, from eight in the morning till five or six at night. The summer was his time to rule. I don't know who trained him but I can tell you he was hard. He was building a lean mean fighting machine. I was his number one pupil that he was well pleased with. I always try to please my superiors. Push—ups, sit-ups, wrestling, boxing, knife fighting, hand to hand combat, bail-outs, and flight training. Which all were done on a daily basis. They moved from Houston, Texas to Detroit, both large cities. Sergeant Rod was an expert in many skills, boxing, wrestling, football, baseball, hockey, and gambling. I don't know if he was under orders, or he took it upon himself. Maybe it was his duty, or this is just what he was created to do. He took me through everything he knew step by step. Second in command was my brother Corporal Con he was in charge of tactics and missions. He was easy going smart and very laid back. Always reading everything he could absorbing all information.

My mother and father enjoyed working. When we first moved here my mother's sister came with them and she helped with the children. When she moved out of town opened up the possibility that we would be home alone. Being the oldest and strongest my brother Sergeant Rod would exert his authority. Training would start early in the morning. He would train me all day for breakfast lunch and dinner, only to be stopped when Lt. Abrams got home in the evening. My father was a drill sergeant in the United States Air Force and retired as a Lieutenant Navigator, now he works at the armory in Detroit.

Chapter 2

GROWING UP IN DETROIT

I GREW UP IN DETROIT, Michigan, AKA The Motor City, at the height of its glory, in the 1950's. This city has always had a special magic for me. In the air was the smell of maple leaves, cherry blossoms, and wild flowers. The city put a line of maple trees on our street and one was right in front. Across from our house was a older house with many fruit trees, grape vines an a cherry tree. When I grew up the music I heard while in our house was like the atmosphere

"Ooooooooooooooooh Oh Baby love, I need your love" sung by Diana Ross, or Sam Cooke waiting by the docks, the Beatles singing "I want to hold your hand" or " Money can't buy Love" and Little Stevie Wonder doing "clap your hands just a little longer," and " I found love on two way street and lost it on a lonely highway". I heard all this and more on the radio. The words it took me a while to understand but the music was beautiful in the air. My mother or brothers would play music in the morning.

When my father would get in at night he would play Jazz and Classical music, like Bach, Brahms, Dizzy Gillespie, or Louis Armstrong. My father had a nice record collection. He had some Japanese music that was on 78 speed. Music was a regular part of my life.

The manufacturing plants created by Henry Ford, put a car in every household, and sped up the transportation, and farming industry. Mass Production and Detroit saved the free world, when they changed the car factories into tank and airplane assembly lines to win WWII. Barry Gordy and the Supremes created the Motown Sound by using Detroit talent and Detroit autoworkers, to become one of the largest records selling company still being heard around the world. Albert Einstein created the theory of relativity, $E=MC2$ this is when I knew I wanted to be a scientist. When President Kennedy commissioned the race to the moon, I guess I was swept up into becoming an Astronaut. I was a patriotic American who wanted to give my life for my country, I like most Americans Loved our President. In every home from my grandmother's, to great aunt, their was always a picture of President Kennedy. We all loved America and was ready to serve our country.

My father sat watching as he was elected this was very important in our house. My Father was also a patriotic American and a United States Air Force officer, now working for the city of Detroit.

I was raised in a regular American family in the fifties. After dinner we would go from the kitchen table to the bathroom to wash, then to the living room floor. We would sit with my father and mother to watch television the whole family. The television was a new invention. We used to sit at the radio to hear the comedy shows, but the television now gave American families time to be together. We had our shows we would watch regularly like; the Mickey Mouse Show, Howdy Dowdy show, Bozo the clown, Soupy Sales show, Batman, Bugs Bunny, and Popeye cartoons, my parents would have theirs, Ed Sullivan, Perry Mason, and Bonanza. Some shows would be for families and we would all be in the room together. This was a time where we could get my fathers attention. One thing I never saw in our house growing up was my mother and father kissing and loving each other. I could see their Love for each other. My father was very conservative an intelligent gentlemen with class. They didn't have many arguments that I heard. My father held his feeling till they got to their bedroom. Yes they had disagreements but they worked things out together. My mother would campaign for the things she wanted and then make deals with restrictions. She wanted to give us everything we needed to become the leaders of tomorrow. My fathers upbringing was very regimental and religious so his displays of affection were very limited. My father would play his Bill Cosby album and we all would laugh. He had a good sense of humor. One time I asked my father a question that I was thinking about. "Dad when how will I know when I'm in Love." He looked at me and fell out laughing. He had a high loud different laugh. Then he said "You'll know". My father was always giving out orders it wasn't much of the nice Lt Abrams. My mother on the other hand was always nice and practical. Trying to meet the needs of the whole family and doing it equally. My mother was always talking to us about everything, helping to shape us and yes even my father.

My earliest memory is of waking up for breakfast washing our face and going to the table. Our mother made us oatmeal with raisins, brown sugar, butter and toast. Who arrives first is very important, every good spy knows never eat without seeing when it was placed. We start eating our food. When we get finish Sergeant Rod informed Corporal Con his food was poisoned. Rod said to Con "I spit in your food." Con jumps up hacking and runs to the bathroom trying to spit it out in the toilet. Con then demonstrates the process to bring up any poison. By sticking out your tongue and putting your fingers down your throat till all food come out. Sergeant Rod is always trying to make us better meaner leaner fighting machines, he knew no bounds. Rod was in the Core four years Con only two I was the new rooky. I don't know their history but I do know that they trained in Houston Texas, and just moved to this barracks. It's clear to see that Con was the brains and Rod the muscle and they had bad blood between them. I was use to this because it was always happening, Rod enjoyed torturing him. This all started before me and had something to do with brother rivalries. It started in Texas, Houston were my older brothers were born. My thoughts are that Lt. Abrams taught the core and they were teaching down line to me a new recruit. I am sure there were things that Sergeant Rod couldn't get Corporal Con to do. He was impressed with my abilities, and desires to learn more. He must have had former problems with the Corporal, but we had no problems until I started to take sides with the Corporal. I found out that the Corporal was much weaker than Sergeant, but smarter and kinder. The Corporal would read anything he put he hands on from comic books, magazines, books, to newspapers and engine manuals. Many times we would go to the mobile library to get our supplies. In there we could learn about anything. Sergeant just worked out all the time, throwing footballs and baseballs, running, playing hockey, he was very athletic. I learned both of these areas but at the time I was only interested in athletic activities not reading or writing. Rod was one of the best in the area, there was only one problem. The Sergeant distasted authority with a passion. Being the first born he had many run ins with Lt. Abrams. I can only guess what happen early on but I heard stories of growing up in Houston Texas. How he was loved by the whole neighborhood. The son of their favorite southern belle one of Walter Haller daughters Renee. She was the cat meow light skinned beauty with green eyes and long curly reddish blonde hair. She wasn't just beautiful, she was also intelligent and talented. I guess I'm prejudice cause "that's my mama". She worked on the Air Force Base as a cashier in the cafeteria, and drove a Ford convertible. She was very popular along with her sisters and loved by many. Many times she would sneak out and go to the beach where they would light a fire and cook crabs on the bay. Sergeant Rod could get away with almost everything while in Houston. His Grandfather and Grandmother who loved him very much, begged Renee to let him stay with them. I understand why Sergeant is so intense and driven. To be taken from an environment while still developing can be stressful. Then to go from saint who can do no wrong to villain who is the cause of all the problems. In Texas he was a hero but here in Detroit he's a white boy and a target for endless abuse. In a city where most of the negro's were brown skinned with dark eyes and dark hair. He stood out like a sore thumb. All throughout school he fought from sun-up to lunch, and didn't stop till recess. Maybe that's why he never stayed in school. Maybe that's why I had to be so tough. I was a reflection of his training, to become a great soldier. Corporal Con on the other hand excelled in school, absorbing all he could put his hands on. He went to the top of his class and was double promoted twice. Some thought he was a genius. Sergeant Rod knew he was not and set out to prove this fact. This is when I forged my friendship with Corporal Con. I started standing up for his rights. I made a choice between Power and Knowledge, Good and Evil.

This was the beginning of a battle and this was the fight of my life. I never won but I've always done my best. Sergeant Rod was a strict disciplinarian and a thorough trainer. Many times I would get thrown in a wall, or busted my head through a window. I would wrestle my brother everyday when I would lose he would ask me to give up. He found out that I would never give so he created a finishing move to declare he won. This is when he would put he knee on my scrotum and apply pressure. I still wouldn't give-up. I told him the next time he tried that move I would urinate on him. The next day he tried his new submission move. I used all my power to summon my fluids out on his knee. It wasn't until he felt the wetness on his knee, that he flew into a wild rage. He punched me a few times and threw me around like a rag doll. While calling me a nasty ____ ____ ____ and dragged me around the house. Then he went to the bathroom and started running water, scalding hot water. He came back and dragged me to the bathroom. He was trying to push me in the tub filled with hot water when my mother drove up and saved me. He told me "you little worm, I will beat the ____ out of you. I'll will kick your ass every time I remember of what you've done. If anyone ever reminds me of this I will kick it again." Yes he held to his word, but he knew I would still defy him again. I don't know why I went against the Sergeant. I just didn't like the way he tortured the Corporal and I. I would be much stronger if I stuck with him. I learned everything from my brothers.

I never knew how this had an effect on my development. My choice on who I would become started here coward, hero, good or evil. Though I was the younger child I would stand between my older brothers to stop the fights. At about five or six I started standing up against Sergeant Rod. I would get my ass kicked just for trying, I learned at an early age, trying to stop evil could be painful. There was something inside that always picked me up and kept coming back for more never giving up. Sergeant Rod had to admire my spirit or something because he started giving me a break. He felt that he was getting me ready for the world. To tell the truth I would not be the man I am today if it was not for him.

Flight practice was my favorite class. I always wanted to fly from as early as I could remember. I would try anything that would simulate that experience. I would jump out of swings at the height of the revolution, that's what we called "bailing out" and I was the bail-out king. I'd love climbing trees, jumping off houses, and garages. One day while we were playing king of the hill, Sergeant Rod picked me up on the top of the pile of dirt and threw me into a newly dug basement of a new house. This is first time we did this maneuver but I was always ready for my training. Although on the way down I thought I was flying, time stood still and I flew like superman. When I hit the bottom hard, the dirt knocked the wind out of me. As Sergeant Rod begged me not to tell as he took me back home to the base. He asked me why I didn't try to land on my feet. All I could do was throw up all my lunch on my way home. I was quite a dreamer, I was flying, I was finally airborne. Why did I want to fly so bad, why did I want to be an Astronaut so bad. I just loved heights and being high up in the air felt good to me. Maybe my training had something to do with it, or maybe Corporal Con wanting to be a Scientist started me think of Space. Maybe I just wanted to go somewhere peaceful. I never understood why I was being trained. I thought this was just life. I'm sure there were many kids who went through training of their own.

On weekends we would catch the bus downtown to play checkers at the top of the fisher building. Because I was the youngest they had to take me with them. On one trip I learned simulated poison control training. We would take the Eight mile bus to State Fair Grounds then take the Woodward bus downtown. While on the bus Sergeant Rod dared me to drink all the hot sauce out of a pork rinds bag. I was good at dares and I would take all dares. I tore open the package that held the hot sauce and dumped in my mouth. My eyes bucked wide open as the sauce burned my mouth. I was ready to spit it out but that's when Sergeant Rod grabbed me by the throat and said " swallow it, Swallow it, Now, Don't spit it out!". I did, it tore out my insides burning all the way down. It kept burning in my stomach for a while, next thing you know we were there. The Fisher building and other huge buildings would go up so high in the sky. Looking to the top of these building from outside was amazing. We would tilt our heads all the way back to see them. In the sixties Detroit had an modern thriving business district, with many people walking back and forth. The streets were wide with cars three deep on each side. The cars were moving up and down through the streets. These huge metal machines were all painted like pictures decorated with chrome, glass lights, wide doughnut whitewall tires, all looking original. Streetcars looked like an open train cart with seats and a conductor in the front. It had wires on top that ran with the track up and down some major streets. Down the middle of the street was an island with grass, trees, flowers, that made the smell in the air sweet. When we got inside it looked like we made to the city of Oz. The floors were marble, the wall marble decorated with gold inlay. They had huge chandeliers hanging from the super high ceilings with pictures on them. The elevator doors were large six in a row on both sides. We loved elevators every chance we get we would ride one.

At this time we were living at Griggs and 8 mile. We just moved from Tyler street by 12th, close to the Northend. There were many new brick homes built for black migrate workers from the south, by the government for five grand each. From Birwood to Livernois right behind Outer Drive was where they put them. 8 mile is the border of Detroit there were other older homes around ours, but it use to be an all white area. This was the poor outskirts of the city other homes built earlier in Detroit are far superior than these. Just a half mile to the south was the middleclass of Detroit. There were much nicer brick homes for large families from 7 mile to 6 mile. North from Livernois were smaller mansions for wealthier households. They were built from 1920 to 1935. At this time Detroit is a strong city and everything outside of it limits is much weaker economically. But 8 mile was and still is a strong business street, because it is the borderline of Detroit territory. On the other side of was Oak Park, Royal Oak Township, and Ferndale. Royal Oak Township became a predominate black area, while Oak Park and Ferndale stayed mostly white. The leaders of those cities fought to keep their statutes and culture the same. In the early 20's and 40's Black's could only live in Black bottom, or Paradise Valley. There is a history of well to do black families that moved into all white good neighborhoods and went through cruelness and many were killed. After legislation pasted that stopped segregation opened up the cities to become populated by other nationalities. City taxes could be the catalyst that started many white families to move to the Suburbs.

Because they started moving before legislation had pasted. This time the suburbs were mostly farmland, the money and power of Detroit turned them into new economically strong cities While in turn changed Detroit into the new Black Ghetto. This whole area just ten years ago was all white. Our house cost five thousand dollars, which my grandfather gave to my father, so that he could have a house built in Detroit.

In fact they had a wall that separated colored from living on one side of it. Detroit like other cities had certain areas that colored could live, which was changed when they made a nondiscrimination clause in real estate. In the sixties all this changed when we got civil rights. Realtors used this to make more money by Blockbusting, getting people to move out of areas where blacks were moving to in Detroit. They would call homeowners and tell them that blacks were moving in and it would made their property values drop. When we moved there it was the beginning of the white flight, not just our area, but all over the city whites started moving out at a fast pace. This is when the suburbs were built which offered new homes outside of Detroit, but these home's weren't better than the homes built in the 1920's to the 1950's. At the time when most of the homes were built between those times they had large work forces of specialty worker. The Craftsmanship that was used at that time and the materials was much better because the cost of them was much lower. The reality is that the homes built in Detroit were constructed better than the homes in the suburb which were inferior but cost more. Construction crews of 20 to 30 were replaced by crews of 5—10 workers. As time goes on construction cost rise, as the value decreases, where the older homes were built better and last longer. Like they say you pay for the location not the house itself. This lead to all the vacant homes in Detroit it was about making money. The realtors made more money to sale homes in the suburbs.

When they talked someone to move out of Detroit, they would get a double sale. One for the house they left, and another for the new home sale. This is another reason why Realtors in this area got bad names as a slick cheaters, and dishonest businessmen.

The year was 1957 and across the street was a large vacant field and a concrete wall, which separated Birwood from Mendota. This was a segregation tool of the past. Although I never saw any white people jumping over it. We called it the Mendota wall we never knew that it was used to keep whites apart from Negroes. The kids living over the wall would run us off the field many times all of them were darker and wilder. We called them the Mendota boys and they were a strong gang that would take over the field whenever they wanted. I lived on Griggs street sixteen years, and became the leader of the Griggs Street gang. All the strong families were known by their lasts names and there were five to seven children in each family. These families would run the streets; there was the Moon family, the Browns, Thornton family, Rose family and my family the Abrams, all on Griggs, while the Wilson's lived on Mendota. Their were other families but these were the leaders of the streets. The first born from the family made a mark on the street from their intelligence, strength or courage. That name would live to protect the other brothers and sisters in that family. We lived by reputation on the street and tales of what was done were kept by word of mouth. Their was always a competition to be the best, the fastest, the strongest, in all sports, cars, and even the toughest dog held a place.

The Wilson's were the strongest family across the wall, the oldest brother was Donnie a golden gloves champion boxer and his brothers Glen and Doll-baby the baby boy. They won many awards boxing and were famous in Detroit along with Tommy the hit man Hearns. Our street had five of the strongest families on 8 mile on one block. The Moons were the top family with Ricky the oldest, a young genius that was to intellectual for the school system which became the leader of the street gang. Theresa was his strong lieutenant. Although she was a female, she was still stronger than many guys and also very smart and cocky. Marva was the oldest, and Elaine and Deborah were the youngest and finest girls on the block. The Browns were the strongest family the oldest Larry was a football star, that went to college to play football. He was a track star also, as was most of the Browns. Alton was the second oldest then Derrick, Cheryl and Felicia and they had an older sister. One day I fell for Cheryl. She was so fine and had the most beautiful shape and pretty eyes and face, chocolate brown with the roundest behind I had ever seen. Just looking at her did something to me, I was never able to say anything to her because I had not learned how to talk to girls yet. The Rose family was strong also, four boys and one girl, the older sister would watch my back as a kid, Denise, we called her Dochie. She would ride me on the handlebars of her bike. They had the meanest dog on Eight mile and he could beat any dog around. Ronnie, Glen, Mail, and Lanny were the boys. Lanny and I were best friend for years. The Rose boys won many street fights and had respect in the streets. The Thornton family was not big fighters but they were street smart. The older brother Lovett was a real slick hustler. His younger brothers was Steve and Mike they were not as bad as the other families but we all became friends, they had some younger sisters also. Our Neighbors the Danzys had four girls and they lived right next door. Belinda was the oldest, then, Gayle she was my age, and two younger sisters Beanie and Robyn. Then the Abrams family was mine, my older brother Rod was called White-boy because he was very light skinned and had sandy brown hair and green eyes. This was not a compliment in fact it was an insult, and caused him many fights. Bobby was a brown skin bully who was like Rock-Bottom on "the Felix the Cat" cartoon. Bobby who lived on Birwood across from the playground would call him whiteboy almost everyday. Every time Rod would run catch him and beat him down. This is one of the reasons he was so tough. Rod was one of the strongest and wildest on the street. He was the strong arm to Rickey Moon's gang, whose mother died at an early age and they had to raise themselves. Theresa took over as mother of the family, their house was the hang-out for everyone cool. Rod had the gift of winning most fights, card games and was a excellent cheater, cat burglar, and thief. My second brother Con was very smart he was double promoted twice and could play any instrument from woodwinds, to electric guitars. Then me, Duane, jack of all trades master of none, my twin brother D, twin sister, and a baby sister. My younger brother D was another musical genius who could play anything by just hearing it on the church piano. He started with drums but grew to own a studio and played keyboards. My sisters were also some of the finest on our street.

Detroit was changing with the new jobs for Negro workers attracting many people to this city to raise their families with a decent job. All the workers didn't just work for the car companies, the city itself hired many positions with good decent pay, the police department, the fire department, the water department, sanitation department, parks and recreation all were better jobs than in the south. So many came from the south that Detroit became more black than any other big city. My father started working in the accounting department and moved up to the budget department, then to director of city DPW, and ended up controlling the city when Mayor Coleman Young became ill in his last term.

The area we moved to used to be all white, but they started moving to the newly built suburbs, by way of the newly built freeways. Detroit at the time had a large Negro community that's what we were called back then, Negro.

Negroes could only live in either black bottom or Paradise Valley. This was before they built the freeway right down the middle of it. After changing discrimination legislation and building the freeways through Black Bottom and Paradise Valley, blacks started moving all over the city. This ended many black owned businesses, and churches that had to be relocated.

While the change was happening the schools had mostly white teachers with few black teachers. The area changed before the teachers had a chance to relocate. I went to Higginbotham Elementary school on Chippewa across Wyoming. It was a well developed public school with programs like most suburban schools have now. My kindergarten teacher was Mrs. Sales a brown skinned lady with large black curls in her hair, always wearing colorful dresses with designs on them. The sweetest, nicest lady, I had ever met with never a loud tone but stern, the classiest woman you could ever meet. My first grade teacher Mrs. Hargrove the kindest lady, my band instructor Mr. Cross, and my sixth grade English teacher Mrs. Date a Jewish lady that almost when blind trying to read my Hieroglyphics. My writing skills must of been developed in Egypt, under the rein of the great black Pharaohs. This school formed the my early education even though some things that were taught I questioned. These teachers taught me many things and the one that stands out the most was the overlying theme " You can do anything you want, even become the President of the United States." Maybe it was my old elementary school Higginbotham that inspired me to reach for the sky. I believed that I could do anything that I wanted to, and work in any field that I desired. I believed what I was taught.

At an early age I was always trying to help, at home with my mother, brothers, and sisters, stopping fights between my brothers and helping my mother cook, sometimes at the risk of getting hurt myself when going against my older brother. Sergeant Rod taught me how to fight and that meant that I got my ass kicked while learning. He would tell me that if I didn't beat whoever I was fighting, then he would kick mine when we get home. One day he made me fight my best friend Lanny, just to prove to his friends that I was the best.

We had said that we were going to be Scientist, Corporal Con and I. He showed me how to make a rocketship out of Christmas ornaments. We lived by vacant lots, with tall uncut grass, which came in real handy for us. All the kids on our street enjoyed these vacant lots, they were excellent for play areas. We used them for our science labs, and play areas, where we could collect, bees, grasshoppers, crickets, ants, squirrels, and worms. The lots across the street from our house on Griggs street were there from the twenties. An old woman lived, in an old model wood frame house on one of the lots there were two other houses on it also but mostly vacant land. There was a fire in that house and she moved and it was left vacant for a while, then the field was filled with long tall grass and tall trees. The grass was so tall that you could get lost in it. We loved playing in it, hiding there, playing army, and climbing trees. My first science experiments were done there, my older brother wanted to be a scientist, so that's what I wanted to become. He would take wooden match heads, and put them in old Christmas ornaments and shoot them in the air. One day I was in the field by myself and I stuffed my rocket full of match heads. After getting my rocket ready I did my countdown and lit it. It took off as I watched it fly and hit the ground then it started to burn the grass all around. It spread so fast, I backed up a little, then I tried to put it out by stomping on it, but it was too late. The wind blew, and it spread too quickly for me to stop it, the fire grew fast, so I ran home. The whole field was now completely on fire, people started coming out to look, and called the Fire Department. Back then the Detroit Fire Department had a fire box system, on the streets in Detroit. They would have a Fire Box with a number on it with the location. It was a red pole with a box number on the corner of a street a red box with a white lever in it behind a glass door. Ours was on the corner of Griggs and Norfolk. As time went by things changed. Too many false alarms changed the system. The Box alarms were discontinued on the street corners. They still use the box number system, but only to give the location. Some schools and factories still use the box system. No one ever found out that I set that fire, and I never told anyone. Maybe I never saw any Fire Trucks when I was younger because I was always running away from them. The second thing I thought of was my best friend Junior Scott, who would pull false alarms just for fun, and start running. We'd be walking and just to add a little fun Junior would always have to do something. He would either pull a fire alarm, or throw a brick in someone window, preferably a well to do home. I just found out that's what he use to do when we started hanging out. Maybe that's why I never saw a fireman, because I was too busy trying to run away and hide. When we started hanging out I stopped them from destroying peoples homes. Just for fun if we would see the police we would start running just to get them to chase us. The things we did for fun were crazy. At the time we were allowed the burn our trash, and leaves in our backyard. I loved looking and playing in the fire. Every time we'd barbeque I was there for starting the fire, we had a home made pit made of bricks. I would love to watch the fire and help get it started. One day we were getting the fire started and my older brother had a large fork for turning the food. Bravery training was to stand in the mouth of danger and not flinch. Sergeant Rod had a test where he would swing at me with a stick or stab at me with a knife and I couldn't move. I got so good that no matter what he would do, I wouldn't flinch. One day he was stabbing at me with the BBQ fork, I didn't move. I guess this wasn't good enough for him so he stabbed harder. Well that fork went right through my arm and it was stuck there. "Don't tell, don't tell" he asked , I went straight for my mother when it was time to seek medical attention. I held the prize for going to the hospital and getting more stitches than anyone else in the hood. Doctors amazed me they could just sew up and repair the skin so easily. I loved science and was interested in becoming a surgeon.

All my Life I have made a quest for Super Powers. In my early years I wanted to fly, I think it's every young boys wish to fly, so every chance I got I tried it. Climbing trees swinging from tree to tree, riding a playground steel swing sets accelerating to the maximum height and jumping out flying thought the air seemed natural. My brothers and some of our friends that lived on our street would climb to the top of our one story ranch home to get the sun. I just loved climbing up and jumping off. After watching the daily superman television show started my quest not for just the power but to fight against crime, cruelty, and justice. My fascination grew to airplanes and rocket ships, which opened my mind to the world of science. I don't know what's in me that made me reach for the heavens. Magic was the next great wonder to see something pop out of thin air that was not there a second ago. Television producers came out with a hit show "Bewitched" which showed people with the power to create and manipulate people and situations with witchcraft. Then came Star Trek another series that showed our future of traveling to different worlds and displaying a new culture of all races getting along. Entertainment has to gift to make reality seem real, more importantly it can make us reach for a better future. A future with peace, justice, prosperity, in a high tech world, where we would be fighting aliens, not other earthlings. My Quest is to fight for the best possible future for our world. I learned my themes and goals from school, and the television programs. School, Art, and

Entertainment had programs that set up positive themes and goals for a better world. The music was played on the radio heard all over the city had another influence on popular life. When the city changed the music did also. The street taught me other lessons of negative behavior while showing me how to survive from street game, and other destructive forces.

Parents need to talk to their children about relationships what happen back in the 50's helped us to be a better family. After coming out of slavery we had the choice to marry who we wanted, after living in America we have accepted their ways. The Jewish people keep their culture, the Arab nations keep theirs, so did the Polish, and Irish, why do my people simulate their captures. We need to recapture our culture, and rebuild new ways to keep our families together.

My very first girlfriend was Gayle, she lived next door I was four, and she called me Waynie-boy. Lanny lived three houses down from us and we played together all the time. These were my friends for life, Lanny a young pretty boy, from the start my mother though he was a girl because of his long pretty hair, that was dark and wavy. We played in fields of wild flowers, we would play army in the dirt, and make mud pies, then catch bees and grasshoppers together . Gayle on the other hand loved playing house and having tea parties. She knew way more about everything. We would go to sitting on the porch with Gayle, and this was heaven, she was more advanced then us. She would read Mary Poppins and other books while we would gaze into the sky thinking. Disney Tales were our favorite stories and she would read until it got dark and we had to go inside. The girls that went to school with her had my heart, they went to a Catholic school, while we went to a Public School. Education makes a big different to a child, what they were taught in Catholic school compared to what we were taught in Public school. That right there would of made a big different to my life. After we both grew up even though we stopped talking as much after we became teens, we were still very much alike. We believed in some of the same things, our goals were the same, and our mission in life was the same. That was helping people, looking after children, and not just thinking and planning but doing something about it. My mother was a den mother for the boy scouts, I was a cub scout, we went to many outings and banquets. The scout award services were held in the school gym at Higginbotham annually. I learned many things from the Scouts, including how to swim, tie rope knots, out door cooking at a camp fire, how the be respectable, honest, trustworthy, this was the correct way to raise children. The churches, schools, businesses and many of the families on our street were involved in theses actives in the fifties. (What happen to these type of programs, why are they not in the city, were they also budget cuts?)

The first pain I felt for a girl was Jerry. She was a beautiful mixed girl. Her father was black and her mother was Pilipino. She had long brown hair, and we were friends. I thought she was fine. Everyday on the way home she would always kick me in the shin. This was awfully painful. I told Corporal about her and he told me that they were love taps. This was a very strange way of showing one that they liked you. I would of done anything to have her as a girlfriend, but as it turned out she never spoke to me again. The Corporal devised a way I could find out if she did like me. It was very simple, the form letter. I would write on a piece of paper; I like you, do you like me, followed by three empty boxes with the words written on the side, yes, no, maybe. I gave Jerry, the letter and I waited to find out the answer. We were in Art class and as always she was kicking me under the table, in the shins with her wooden Dutch shoes. Well this time in art class she kicked me so hard I fell out my chair and let out a scream" Ouch." The teacher didn't think it was love taps, in fact because we disturbed the class, and we were sent to the office. Now I never got in trouble for anything this was the first. We waited in the hallway for the assistant principle. I had no idea what was going to happen. We never got in trouble before, I thought he was just going to talk to us. I was wrong the assistant principle gave both of us a paddling. No words, no expiation, just paddlization.

He wasn't playing, it was a large paddle with holes in it. The gym teacher Mr. Johnson had one too. They displayed them like they were trophies. Actually the paddles were sharp, they had decorations with writing and painted sayings on them. Jerry's family moved away not long after that. That incident could have been the cause of her moving. If my daughter got paddled over something that insignificant I would be very upset. Back in those days they were very regimental. In those days they didn't take any stuff off the children in school. Today they would have the parents sit down and talk about the problem. Not many parents had the time to take off from work to check with the teachers. The teachers were more powerful and had discipline power to paddle children they felt went against their rules. Now I had sore shins and a sore rear end!

I have always thought of her as that beautiful young girl with ponytails. Part Black, part Asian with the prettiest eyes. She looked like Lucy Lu, as a little girl. This could have been my ultimate soul mate if I could have stopped her from kicking me. We were eight years old, going to Higginbotham Elementary. She was a shy silent type just like me. All I felt was held deep inside. Jerry just kicked out the way she felt the only way she knew. If only she could of said something.

My role models were Jerry Lewis and Dean Martin, this is who I wanted to grow up to be like. Funny like Jerry and cool like Dean with all the chicks. I always bragged about having five girlfriends or more but never had one. Gayle knew more about a real relationship than I did, their mother and father showed their affection for each other on a daily basis. I never saw or heard anything like that in our house. I learned about relationships from television, movies and the streets. In my heart, the first girl that I wanted to marry was the pretty little girl with the two long ponytails that kicked me under the table in my Art class. Jerry, Jerry . . . , I can still feel the pain on my shin. The vice principle gave us a smack on the rear end, my rear end hurt then, but now only my heart hurts because of the lost love I never knew. This was the best sign to show me, Love was out to hurt me.

Then the night I will never forget when Hilda the princess of the ball, the finest girl in the area invited me to her birthday party. She was super fine and intelligent too. She liked me enough to invite me to her birthday party. This event was like the Grand Ball from the Cinderella fairy tale, not everyone was invited. My mother dressed me up and bought her a present. I thought no girl even knew me, this made me feel good just to be invited. Her house was flawless, like a castle, the party was impeccable. They had party hats, pin the tail on the donkey, and a beautiful cake, and when it was all over. We sat in her backyard on her swing set talking with her girlfriend Cassandra. I was sitting alone talking, with the homecoming Queen, and she seemed interested. That day changed my life when I found out that girls liked me. Not just any girl but a classy smart one had a crush on me. I knew they liked Lanny because he was the finest guy in our neighborhood. The girls were crazy about him like he was a movie star. Girls were always talking about Lanny and he was my best friend. He was the prince, I was the court jester.

The girls who stole my heart were Hilda, Cassandra, and Peggy, all nice smart girls from school. I was scared of the girls with the bad reputations. They were very pretty but all the bullies, thugs, and pretty boys got them. I was just a regular kid that didn't know much about girls. I wasn't taking chances on being embarrassed. I heard stories of the girls getting humped in the doorways, or in the bathroom at the school. I did not understand what was happening. Why were girls getting humped. What was humped? Many things I didn't know, so I didn't worry about them.

The Corporal and I went on many adventures without the Sergeant. When the Corporal was double promoted he was chosen to become a Safety Patrol Boy. I became a cadet safety patrol boy to help him. We were given special privileges. We could leave early, fifteen minutes before school was out. That would give us time to get to our corner before any children had to cross the street. The Corporal was given a bright orange safety patrol belt that would cross from our shoulder across our chest and then around our waist. The corner we were given to protect was Norfolk and Wyoming. Norfolk was a side street but Wyoming was a main street with 30 miles per hour traffic, and no stop light. This was a very important assignment because their were many accidents on this street. One day a man on a motorcycle lost his head. We saw his head in a helmet on the side of the street bleeding. We took our job very serious and we enjoy the authority that came with our service. Corporal Con got the job first, he just brought me in to help him later. We were entrusted with the safety of all the children that walked that way home. "Hold up" means stop, "let's go" means they can cross the street. Everything went well for a while until we ran into a troublemaker. He was a light skinned, heavy set young man with a bald head. When he got closer to us instead of walking across with everyone he jay walked to the other side of the street. Then he ran across Wyoming and went home. The Corporal reported him and the next time we were ready. The next day we were at our corner when he tried to do the same thing. As soon as he darted across the street Corporal shouted get him. I took off after him and caught him. He put up a fight but I was stronger. I walked him across the street, and he crossed the street with the other children the correct way. Everyday he would try us but we were too clever for him. We ended up babysitting him they lived on Birwood right by eight mile, his mother was beautiful. She looked real similar to our mother, light skinned, long light brown hair, light, pretty eyes. Her son was always getting in trouble and she wanted us to keep an eye on him for her. The Corporal had other young men that we would sit for in the neighborhood. When we got older the Corporal needed more money and sitting wasn't making enough. After asking around about making money he heard about the newspaper boys.

At that time The Detroit News northwest regional route office was in the alley behind, 8 mile between Wyoming and Washburn. We went there and met the route manager and he gave the Corporal a route. It was the Ilene, Griggs, Birwood route and it was nine city blocks. One of our friends, Lovett, who lived down the street had one too. We would go get our papers together after school. We made friends with most of the other paperboys that went to our school. We were given a list of people that received the paper on our two streets. The Corporal figured it out to making thirty three cent per week per customer. After paying for the papers we made about twelve to fifteen dollars a week. When we got finished delivering the papers we would meet at Brodies Mufflers on 8 mile and Griggs. We would go to Leo's Party Store on 8 mile, to get snacks and hang-out with the mechanics. My favorite snack was a Hostess Suzy Q, Cheese Curls, and a Faygo Red pop, with this in my bag I was happy. I never needed more than that I had nothing else to spend my money on, so I would lend The Corporal and Sergeant money all the time. By delivering papers we would know almost everyone on our street. We met many new people and made many friends, I would end up getting a real girlfriend. This was a nice job to meet girls with, and there is always something most attractive about a man with a job. At this time a girlfriend is just what it should be a good friend. Someone to talk with hang-out, play baseball, and other games. This is when I met a new friend Ronda that lived down by eight mile. Her family moved into a newly built house right behind the muffler shop.

After delivering the papers I would go down by her house to play. She was a very out spoken young lady, she wasn't like the other girls playing with their dolls. She didn't hang with those other girls down the street that were too pretty to even speak. Right behind the Electric Lighting Company we would play baseball. Now this was a girl I could grow to love but she was very complex. She was my age and my size the only difference was our sex. Sex now that's something that never came up cause we were pals. We went head up and she would always try her best to win. She was good, fast, and strong, yes she was a tomboy. I would love going against her, she won many times and didn't like losing. One time things got just a little too rough, and I stopped going down there. I did something that I will never forget, I hurt her. This hurt me deep inside and from that day on I would avoid competition and roughhousing with girls.

The Corporal set me up with a girl next door to his girlfriend. Her name was Darlene and she was a nice girl with a real pretty smile. I used to ride her in my wagon, we were good friends. The news paper game wasn't all we thought it would be. When it came to collecting the money we found out what "come back next week" means. Back in the fifties people were honest but as the sixties came things started to change. I guess if the first bill you can't pay is the smallest is just a sign that troubles ahead.

The Corporal got tired of the paper game and he went on to work at a Gas station. I went on to meet another best friend, Martin, he was like the Corporal. We would go to the theater to watch Batman, and Matt Helm, his father drove the thunderbird that was in the movie. He tried to tell me about girls and what to do. I was interested in hearing the stories, but not ready to try anything. All the pretty girls stayed on Martins street, Birwood, and I would always walk down it when I got a chance, just to look at them. When Martin's family moved he had me to take over his Newspaper Empire. He had put together seven streets Wyoming, Washburn, Ilene, Griggs, Birwood, Mendota, and Manor. We worked it together until he moved away, then I worked it alone. Now this was a large route but Martin was good he did it with no problem. On Sunday it was the hardest day the papers were very heavy, sometime I had to come back twice to get all the papers. This is when I started hiring help, Ronda's younger brother Damon started working with me . He was eager to help and I needed all the help I could get. When people stop paying it wasn't that bad because my route was so large. A few people not paying just meant I was getting paid less. Right under my eyes things changed, people moved out and new people moved in. The type of people changed as the whole city was changing. I had one customer that lived next door to Ronda and after not paying for over a year owed me five hundred dollars. I could tell they didn't have much money by what her children wore. She was a single mother raising five children, so I kept on delivering her the paper. She would tell me every Saturday come back next week. We thought we hit the jackpot at first all that money we collected. The Corporal didn't like that we would have to turn in more than what we could keep. It was more money than I needed so I would end up lending out to either the Sergeant or the Corporal. Although they never once paid me back one red cent. The Corporal did promise to get me his 1965 Mustang. That never happen either. I started delivering the Free Press News I would get up early and Corporal would drive around and sometime I would ride my bike to do my route.

My first kiss was playing spin the bottle at a birthday party down the street at the Moon's house. I was at a birthday party for Elaine, one of the prettiest girls on the street. I kissed a girl when it was my turn. In spin the bottle we took turns, the boys would spin the bottle with girls in a circle, who ever it stopped on would get kissed. I never kissed before and all I saw was on television. When I turned the girl to the side and leaned over to kiss her, everyone fell out laughing to see my little ass try to kiss like I was a grown—up.

Like my first real kiss in North Carolina, that woke up something deep within. My father would go down to North Carolina every year to visit his parents. Mother Nora my father's mother came up on the train and got me one summer. The Train station was a fabulous marble masterpiece people everywhere, moving back and forth. I was about three or four and I went to live there until the winter. At night the kids would gather under those large trees to play kissing games. A young lady named Angie chose me, I hear later that she liked my older brother. That evening she rocked my world, she gave me a kiss that I will never forget. That was my first real kiss! My older Sgt. Rod warned me about those kisses when they stick their tongue down your throat . One day we were out playing games and Angie took me in her arm and kissed me. She slid her tongue down my throat, she woke up some feeling I never felt before. I thought that it was love. I went into another world, I was floating in the air, I saw stars, my head was spinning, as I melted into her arms. I felt love for the first time although they said it was puppy love. I wrote her many letters in the hopes of marrying her, our song was Betcha by golly wow, by the Stylistics. My favorite song about her was by the Rolling Stones the way Mick Jagger would sing Angie, Angie. I would write her many letters professing my love. We wrote back to each other for a few months. Like many young loves she just faded out of the picture. When we went down the next year I couldn't wait to see her again. To my surprise she didn't even try to see me. I went to her house and left a message, I saw her in church and she didn't even recognize me. She didn't even know me, I think she was only trying to get my brother Con jealous. Maybe she thought I was him since we looked so much alike. Puppy love, here one day gone the next.

She was just kissing me to make my brother jealous, or she just like turning out city boys. It was a long time till I was kissed like that again. Still it meant everything to me she rocked my world, the day the earth stood still. It showed me that while I was blown away, she felt nothing, or not much. Girls are strange, they can kiss a boy and feel nothing. She was so advanced, and I was so slow, she left me in the dust.

My grand parents were married for over fifty years and lived together happily without any known incidents to destroy their marriage. My grandmother would fuss all the time but my grandfather just sat in his chair crossed his leg and smiled. Never a cross word I heard from him, he was a Sunday School teacher at his church. He helped build the church and stayed there till he passed. The day he died he woke up and told everyone he was going home, " you are at home" he was told, then he made up his bed and walked in the backyard. He walked past the giant magnolia tree that had huge beautiful flowers on it that gave off a smell of heaven. Then when he was standing under the giant pecan tree he collapsed. I feel that his angel told him he was going home, that morning he was walking with his angel and walked out of his body straight into Heaven. They were both strong church members my grand father at a Methodist Church and my Grand mother at a Baptist Church. They lived together and loved each other until they passed on. What was it that made it work for them, or was it a time when all this was expected. When you married at their time it was forever, no exceptions. When we were down there we couldn't play with no cards or dice they were considered evil. We would just play chess, checkers, or football outside up and down a street that sloped like a huge hill and our house was in the middle.

I was always interested in girls that looked like my mother; light skinned, long hair, green eyes, with Irish— German features like reddish hair and freckles. At the time I had no idea that was what I was doing. They were just the type of girls I liked. At Junior High it was Karen, a fine light skinned, long brown hair, beauty. I was so shy I never told her how I felt. She went for Reggie on the basketball team, an older guy. Karen Gaines the finest girl in Beaubien Jr. High, in my eyes and many others too. We were in all classes together but, I could only look and dream. I don't think I ever spoke to her because I was so shy. Why was I so shy? I think every time I came out with who I really was it was met with distaste. The one time that always comes to my head was the Junior High School Talent Show. My younger brother, Lanny my best friend and William, and I became a band. My brother played the drums, Lanny played the Guitar, William played Bass, and I played the Saxophone. We knew the talent show was coming so we practiced for weeks, and we put a few original songs together. All of us got our own costumes, my mother made us these vest and pants to match. We were like The Earth Wind and Fire Band, just a little younger and we were ready to start our career off. The audition was at the Beaubien JR High, we got all our equipment together and set up on the stage. One Two Three hit it, we played and played , although we thought we were jamming, but the looks on the face of the committee was complete disgust. After we played our songs we were told that we weren't good enough for the show. This is the same place where the Winans first performed, and they brought the house down. The same school where Aretha Franklin's sons Eddie and Clarence Franklin where also enrolled, Berry Gordy's house was right down the street. Stevie Wonder , and Marvin Gaye lived right down the street. After that we put down our instruments and went to other hobbies, or played football, chased girls, we believed what they said about us that we had no talent. I just think they wasn't ready for our new Rock & Roll Funk.

When I got older my brothers weren't around to influence my decisions. I did the things I was made to do, a fighter for justice. I would help stop fights, especially if I was bigger than them and sometimes if they were larger. There wasn't many larger than me. My body grew so large that I stood out. I had a six foot frame and a very muscular build. I guess I looked like I could fight. I was very cocky at times and with the gift of gab I could talk my way in and out of about anything. I always wanted to be a knight in shining armor coming to the rescue of a beautiful woman.

One day my mother asked me to get my sister from school. She had got into a fight and she needed me to help her. When I got to Higginbotham I went in to get her. She was in the office. My sister was known for beating up boys all the time but this time she got in a fight with a girl. Upon leaving on the front courtyard was a of crowd kids. I pushed my way through when I got in the middle I ran into her. My sister's mouth went off "I told you my brother is going to kick you ass." Regina stood in front of me like a brick wall. She was taller than I, and bigger, not fatter muscular. She was from a long line of bullies, her whole family were bullies. I knew her brother Kenny he was a bully. What has my sister got me into, and she wouldn't shut up for a minute. I had one trick up my sleeve. I first tried diplomacy to get us out of this mess. I had one move if I could bate her into it, so I turned my back on her. She grabbed me in a choke move with her arm around my neck. I grabbed her arm and bent over flipping her over my head. Then I jumped on her and held her down pinning her. After she calmed down I got up and took my sister home. I don't know if my mother knew what she was sending me into, but I made it out the victor. My mother knew she could count on me whatever I had to do, that's why she sent me.

When I started getting older to get me out of the area she would take me with her when she was working for Michigan State, 4 H club. Now this was an organization that helped raise farmers children like the boy scouts.

Every year we would go the Davisburg Country Fair, my mother would be at work while I had the run of the place.

I was in a few fashion shows with my mother being a seamstress their were many shows. This is when many people that worked with my mother found out she was black. When they saw me they would stare and whisper, it wasn't that she was saying she was white. My mother looked white and not just that but she was beautiful also and everyone loved her. I could get a golf cart and ride around, I met a lot of new white people and they weren't bad.

This is when I noticed white girls began to be interested in me. A few young ladies at that fair had a crush on me, the Dingee sisters. There was one big problem, I was black and they were white, although her family was very nice to me and they invited me over. I enjoyed their ranch they had some nice horses. I got to ride the big red one and he was no joke. He kept on wanting to go back to the barn, but when we got farther away he was cool. I enjoyed riding through the fields and by the lake this was something new for me. When I was younger, although I had little experience with the opposite sex. I began to learn a lot when I started working at a summer camp. All of the girlfriends I had there were white, from 4H Camp, the Davisburg Fair, and the camps I used to work through the summer. At 14 and 15 black girls weren't that interested in me, but when I went away to Ann Arbor, Port Huron, and Upper Michigan I was a hit with the white girls. When I went to Michigan State with 4H it was like I was a star maybe because I was the only black guy there. My relationships with the white girls never lasted because of the distance they lived from me and I could only communicate by mail.

I was always good in math, science, and sports in school. Comic books were the only books I would read most of my time was spent doing physical activities. Some days I would play football from sun up till sun down. We would play any team, go to different areas and play other teams. Street football with no pads was life to me and I loved to play everyday I could. I played other sports like basketball, baseball, boxing, swimming, running track, and I was good. This is why I thought I had a chance to join NASA. In my last two years at Mumford high school I raised my C average to A's and B's by graduation in June class of 1975. My Favorite classes were Physics, Trigonometry, Psychology, and Art, which I excelled in the most.

After working two summers as camp counselor, and then resident assistant at MSU days in Lansing, I was picked by friends that worked with my mother. In the summer of 1974 two students from every state were chosen to go to Washington DC, Citizenship Short Course for future leaders. A program set up by the 4H Clubs in connection with Michigan State to enrich teenagers and help them become Leaders and make an informed career choice.

When I went to Washington DC, I met so many beautiful people from all over the United States. There was only a few blacks but many white girls and I was on the hit parade. They were crazy about me not just women but also guys. Friends of my mother selected me for the Citizenship Short Course Leadership training program to open my mind to the business world, nonprofit originations, and a career seminar. We raised money at the county fair to go on the trip. This course had a lot to do with what I became. That week I met so many people the only person that I was set up for to met that wasn't there was my Congressman John Conyers, while everyone else met theirs I didn't. I think he could have instilled a desire to be a Congressman to help change this world.

There was Jan, a beautiful thin white young lady with long blonde hair, who was very intelligent and a good dancer from Boston we went to a formal dance and had a fun night out. I turned the party out with my dance moves, everyone stopped made a circle around us while I put on a show. Back in the day we used to practice all the dances, we had dance routines all mapped out. Like the time we went to my brothers and little sisters birthday party when Dennis Coffee's song Scorpio had a drum solo and when it would start everybody would drop to the floor and do the crawl. We blew that party out and that was what I lived for. I did a different move at the ball and because they played Rock and Roll I did a few other moves like my Turn-around-splits, and my slide walk, it was as if I became the Fonzy on Happy Days.

Then I met Leonardo and Vicky from Michigan, I fell for this beautiful white girl with long wavy hair that had a farm and a horse, and a nerdy tall curly hair sidekick, we went everywhere together. I would call him Leonardo the retardo. We were like Richard Pryor and Gene Wilder and Gilda Raitner , or Eddie Murphy and Steven Martin, we would entertain crowds with our comedy skits. Everybody loved us and we would hang till late at night laughing and telling jokes.

Then I met a young lady from Puerto Rico but I couldn't speak any Spanish. We communicated without language. This was real hard but we had a good time without understanding a word between us. She was tall, thin and with long brown hair we looked alike even though we were from different countries. She was a super fine lady and I wish we could have understood each other. When we couldn't communicate, we would just laugh and smile at each other.

This trip help to build me into a man, I was just seventeen, young, impressionable, and I was molded into what goals and beliefs I used to guide my life. This is when I went to the NASSA research center and why I wanted to join. Seeing the spaceships I knew I wanted to become a pilot. In that setting I was treated as a human and not judged on my color. The other young adults I met were from all different cultures and I was the minority. I feel from this trip I would be treated as an equal, and that was true with everyone my age. The adults were different, this is where the prejudices comes from, it is learned, handed down from generation to generation. The truth of getting this opportunity was only because they needed a black quota for the trip and I was it. I had friends that I didn't know about that like the way I acted. They felt along with my mother that this trip would help me. They were all from Oakland county but I represented Detroit. If I had missed this opportunity Detroit would have been unaccounted.

The confidence I learned help built my character. The different girls from every race that were attracted to me help give me new confidence. This made me want to excel to live the dream. I always felt that my life was important and that I was going to do something big, after this I was validated. After all the bragging about my many exploits now I have finally done something. My claims to be the ladies man with all the girlfriends is now true. Reality set in and maybe I was a big deal in DC but here in Detroit I'm just regular. My gang went to a sweet sixteen party here is where I tried my skills again as the dancer. The mother at the party asked me if I wanted a drink I accepted because I felt like I didn't want to offend her. Every glass she filled of rum straight, I drank, well the only drinking I saw was cowboys, so that's how I drank. She must of thought I wanted more because how quick I drank them. Maybe she wanted to see how many I could drink and still stand. What about they didn't have enough to pay for a clown so just get the young fool drunk and get a free show.

I must have had three glass straight, before I asked the party girl for a dance. I was a born entertainer because everyone there had the best time of their life. Well just like in DC everyone stopped and made a circle around me while I danced. This time it was for shear folly because I was drunk and I was the life of the party. The mother smiled as she watched, others laughed, my friends mouths dropped open wide, as they stared. When we left the party my boys told me of what a fool I was. I said that was the last day I would ever drink again. It was a while before the girls of Detroit treated me like the ones I met in DC. I wrote the girls I met, and dreamed of a better relationship with girls in the city.

That program was a turning point for me, we did a lot of public speaking there, I went to a course at the NASA research center. That's when I made up my mind to join the United States Air Force. My father was a navigator in the Air Force, after graduating from Hampton he became a drill sergeant, then a lieutenant. I guess if I had of understood my father first I could have avoided a lot of problems. Something about the generation gap separated us and I didn't understand that what he wanted was the same that I wanted. My father wanted me to go to college first I wanted to play football, if we could of worked together I might of got it done the same way he did, but I didn't. My father was always working he had at least, three different jobs at a time. He was an accountant for the City of Detroit, at midnight he worked at the Armory, weekends he did Taxes, and sold Kirby vacuum cleaners door to door. My father Conley Abrams worked his way up to be a appointee in the Mayor Coleman Young administration as the Director of Environment and Public Works. My mother Renee Abrams worker for Michigan State University as a home economist and would help low income families learn how to cook nutritious foods with the money they had. She would work with teens teaching them skills like sewing and cooking that would help them develop their skills and talents. I got my spirit to help from her and what I was taught in church. I always loved to help people my friends, family, and even people I didn't know.

My Father told me to go the college but the only way I would of went to college would have been a football scholarship, my plan was to join the Air Force and become a pilot. The truth is I wasn't that interested in certain subjects and always had bad grades in English and Literature. I took all I had to pull up my grades to graduate. I felt I wasn't college material. I was ready to join NASA and, be an astronaut. I asked my mother to take me to the recruiter's office on Grand River and Greenfield. I couldn't wait to join, all I dreamed about was flying. I took the test, and got some good scores, the recruiter told me that my scores were in the eighties and nineties, and it seemed, as he was pleased. He asked me to sit down at his desk, and my mother sat with us. Your scores are real good now what would you like to do. I replied, "I want to be an Astronaut". He opened up his eyes wide, and a great big smile came on his face, and he laughed very loud. He got up and went to the next desk, and told the other recruiter's desk, they all had a good laugh. He came back to his desk and told me I had to grow up, and because I was a negro all I could become is a mechanic. This was my second brick wall, my first passion was football, I loved to play the game, and to be a pro player would have been nice. In the summer we would play football from sun up till it got to dark to see the football. I loved running the ball hitting the holes looking for daylight to run, get in my way I would run you over, I was a hard person to take down, and I thought I was bad. Now I can't become a pilot either, all my dreams hit the floor, and the way he said it I believed him. I though that I could do anything I wanted to. Now as I understand it if I was white I could do anything I wanted to, but because I'm BLACK and don't have a college degree, mechanic is the best I could become. Now two of my dreams were shot down, what will I do now. This is when I learned everything they taught us in school wasn't true.

When we first moved in this new neighborhood had so many beautiful girls I forgot all the girls from my past and school. While just discovering my new street Birchcrest, I remembered when I first saw an angel pass by the front of the house, down the side walk. A super fine young lady everyday at 3:30 she would pass my house. She was a light skinned vision with long light brown hair, I think I was in love the first day I really saw her. She had a small athletic shape wearing blue jeans and a tight fitting blouse. The way the sun would shine on her hair made her look just like an angel from above. I was at the house and the high light of my day was her passing me by. Everyday like clockwork I would be on my front steps from three o'clock waiting to see her again. One day I got up my nerves to speak. I saw her walking down the street to her house. After that I would be waiting everyday same time, same place, to speak to her. She was nice and we spoke often, I was in love with just looks alone she was a dream girl. One day I was driving by in my station wagon and I saw her coming out of her house down the driveway. I pulled my ride over and spoke to her. Her name was Pat and was a tall thin reddish hair with freckles, and a perfect body. She was hot and when we talked she would really invade my space and come real close to my face. We went out a few times, and I met her friend Cynthia. I liked her too she was real nice and we got along. We had real chemistry she was like no other girl I've met. We went out and had many good times. One day I was with her and some of her girlfriends, and I saw her the girl that used to pass my house. I thought she was Pat but, her name was Karen. They looked alike from far off, but up close they were completely different. They all used to hang together Pat, Cynthia, Karen, Denise and Pat, and at one time or another I'd tried to talk to all of them except Denise. Karen , Cynthia, and Denise were sisters, Denise the oldest and smartest of the fine sisters she had long brown hair a little taller and had a caramel complexion and she was the wise owl sister. Cynthia was a brown skinned beauty with a deep Spanish flavor a little heavier with a robust shape a very fun girl who's best friend was Pat from across the street. Then the younger sister Karen, the Angel sometimes when the sun hit her she was drop dead gorgeous. They lived on the next block right off the corner same street as mine. Her hanging partner was her cousin the other Pat. Pat was a little heavier than the others, light brown and she was fine too, but a little tom-boyish. They all hung in a group together I guess to protect each other. When they traveled people would notice four or five beautiful women all drop dead gorgeous. It was just a pleasure to be in their company, I was like a watchdog that would help them if they got in trouble. I hung with them at a few parties, and everywhere they went they would stop men of all types, being taken with the beauty of all of them. I never thought that Karen and I would ever end up together because she was too fine. I still too shy. I was just available to who was smart enough to take control.

My mother got me an application to the Ford Motor Company, Transmission Assembly Plant for the summer. I went in took a test, I was so excited I locked my keys in the car, but with the assistance from a coat hanger I got in. I got the job, with the help from a friend of my mothers. I heard a lot about working in an auto plant. Many of my brothers friends worked for a car company. I heard many stories about working in a auto plant from my brothers and friends on the street. My first job was on the line I would take a part and put it on the transmission while it rode down the assembly line. There were all different kinds of people working there. I met first the senior men that worked there. They taught me how to do the work, and would tell me when all the breaks were how much time I had on each job. Some would have a bottle in their back pocket, and pulled it out when ever the Forman wasn't around. They only just started hiring women again, so there wasn't many there, maybe two or three per shift. There was this one strange guy that would always wear a suits to work Fast Freddie, while everyone else wore work cloths. He danced on Television on channel 62 the Scene. It wasn't much to it you would work for two hours then get a work break then two more hours another break, go to lunch an hour, work two more hours get another break then work two more hours and go home. The company would have to make a Quota (the amount of transmissions they had to make each day) and would stay open until they did. Anytime they had overtime I would take it. If we work overtime we would get paid double time. This would add up to a whole lot of money. I was transferred to midnights and it was nice come in at 12am and work until morning. When I was off I did a lot of hanging and went to a lot of parties all the time. If I didn't go to sleep as soon as I came in I would stay up all day, and then I'd have to go back to work dead tired.

This was the time when I met my first Love, Brenda Starr, she was fifteen and I was eighteen. Now some might say that I was too old but I met her parents, and it was OK with them. I met Brenda hanging out at Butch's house in the basement full of black lights and posters of rock and roll album covers on the walls. We would listen to our records all night long, dancing and singing like we were the stars ourselves. Butch was Jimi Hendrix and I was David Bowie we would perform whole concerts, him with his Fender Stratocaster Guitar, I was doing the vocals. She came over one night with nowhere to go mad about something, and I was just a friend at the right time. After exchanging numbers she asked me to come over on the phone with some records. Her brother said he might know me. I knew it was a couple of guys I used play basketball with lived on her street.

They lived on Mendota street across form the army camp on the other side from where I used to live. The fabulous west side of Detroit by Outer Drive where Stevie Wonder, Marvin Gaye, and Barry Gordy all lived. I walked over her house which wasn't far with my records in my hand. I met her mother and father and they were nice. When her brother came in he saw me and said that's one of the guys that kicked my ass on the playground. I shrank to size of an ant, as I sat on the couch in the living room.

I felt small, and thought that could ruin my love affair, but it didn't.

I became the leader of the Griggs Street gang, because I could beat everyone fighting, and that was always the leader. I stopped all that brick throwing and fire alarm pulling, we just started to look for girls and playing football. I did like saving people I remember one day I was in Junior High. After school some days they had fights and if the girls fought the loser would end up getting her cloths torn off, beaten and kicked, while large crowds would watch. I was just passing the play field and a young girl was being chased by a large crowd. She was small and cute but I had no time to even look. Something hit me and I just ran in a stopped the fight, I told the crowd to leave her along. I had to do some pushing and a little crowd control. I guess being a Gang Boss I thought I was bad, although I was all alone. I ended up walking the girl home. Found out later she was a friend of my sisters. I never spoke to her again but she had told her family what I did for her. Her family was very happy that I stopped that fight.

The day when we played football with her brother I was trying to stop that fight too. I was painted to be a bad guy when we were just playing football with my gang. That day it was Junior Scott , Lanny, My brother D, Anthony, Curtis and I. One player on the other team tackled one of our players real hard. Next thing I knew everybody was going for their weapons. This was our Bruce Lee faze after fighting each other all day long we were ready to fight anyone. We just made some nun chucks and they couldn't wait to try them out on someone. I tried to stop them, " come on you guys stop it leave them alone," but they made that into a joke. While still hitting and kicking them my crew said "Stop leave them alone, Stop". They just keep on fighting, I pulled one of my crew off of a boy. Curtis looked at me and said "yeh leave them alone," all the while he was hitting him. Then everyone else joined in and did the same thing. It was a job keeping my gang out of trouble in fact whenever I wasn't around they would get into real trouble. I heard after I moved Junior Scott joined a gang and became one of the west side Sconey's

When a girl would ask you to come over, all I thought about was just to visit. How shy I was and although I really liked this girl I had no idea what was next. I found out that there is usually something else on sixteen year old girls minds. She was light skinned about 5' 7" a nice thin built, she wore glasses and she looked studious. I was always scared of fast girls she looked like she would take this nice and slow. That's how I worked my magic slow and easy because I don't know anything about relationships. I only lied about having girlfriends and what we were doing. I never really did anything that's why I liked nice girls, but some nice girls are undercover freaks. Take off those glasses let down that hair, and they are wild too. Cat People the movie just came out and she was my new kitten and she loved to play.

On my second visit we played some of my music, Led Zeppelin, David Bowie, Roxie Music, and Kiss. Her mother was cooking dinner her father was reading the newspaper at the kitchen table, and we were in the living room. She would unbutton my shirt, and I would button it back. Then she would unzip my pants and I would zip them back. This was a very exciting game, and I would show my excitement right through my pants. To this very day I can't think of anything more arousing than that time with her, my first love, my Endless Love. The days melted away and four weeks became a lifetime. I met her friends Neskie and the geek squad from Cass Tech everything was swell. We went to the Pontiac Silverdome to see Bob Seger and the sliver bullet band, Todd Rungren, and Kiss with some of her friends. They were real cool, we had a good time, the concert was the bomb. She taught me all about a woman's body and how to appreciate them. We discussed the opinion of the beauty of the breast and agreed that the European held the belief that to fill a champagne glass is perfect. She told me the things she liked and I could only imagine the pleasures. I was just happy to have a friend like her. I dreamed of living the rest of my life with her. I have finally met my soul mate. She was everything I ever wanted, just to sit with her was the world to me. The feeling I felt were like nothing I have ever felt before. Like my first real kiss. Is this love. My father said I would know, this must be it. I was walking on cloud nine for about four good months before the bomb dropped. I saw hints and although my head was in the clouds and I was too happy to notice. What was cool about Brenda was the way she was real and honest with me.

I still saw I might have a problem. She was a little wilder than I thought. One day saw her kissing other boys. She told me they were just friends. The summer was over and so was my relationship. Brenda ended our relationship with a record. She told me to listen to Gino Vanelle's Storm at Sun-up, till this day I can't stand that guy. I guess what it meant was that even though we were hot together, there is a whole world for us to discover.

I had a dream that Brenda and I got married, we were on our way down south to visit my Grandmother in North Carolina. This was just like my father because we would go down south every year in the summer. I felt that there was only one women for every man and that I messed up mine. Now I would have to live alone the rest of my life. I don't know why we were taught with fairy tales. They all lived happily ever after in the stories. I learned real life is quite different.

Now by this time I found out how meaningless that job was. It was just too repetitive, I couldn't be a robot no more. I felt like killing myself that day. I couldn't become an astronaut because I was black. Now the love of my life has broken my heart. I thought of jumping off an overpass to the highway. I remember a friend of ours that climbed to the top of the University of Detroit's radio tower and jumped to his death. My eighteenth birthday was terrible nothing to do no one to see. What is life with out Love.

Riding my bike was the only pleasure I had so I rode to the local Pizza parlor. Two beautiful girls were there flipping pizza dough. This is when then I met Kathy. She worked at Little Caesars with Carmen LaBarrie two super fine ladies. These were our Black Italians dark hair very sexy flipping pizzas. I would just watch her all night, we used to hang out there. Carmen was a fine young lady but she was like a little sister to us. She was so very sexy with her long silky hair and a healthy upper half. This is when I had my chopper Motorcycle. A blue Honda 450 with shorty pipes that used to ring like bells. I lived just to ride that bike everyday, it was so much fun. We all had a bikes like a little gang. I was hanging with Butch and Freddie Dog and we would meet up there almost every day with others from Monica street. I was very depressed, Butch thought it was funny he used to call Brenda, Duck tail soup, because of her age. This was my very first real relationship, although I knew nothing about Love, but I knew I had strong feelings for her. These feelings made me awfully sick, looking at Carmen and Kathy behind the window making pizzas made me feel better. I stayed there after they closed, and asked Kathy if I could give her a ride home. She told me that she was too old for me, and that she was 35years old. I told her how hurt I was because my girlfriend quit me, and felt like killing myself. She let me take her home. I rode her on my motorcycle to her house it was nice ride. It was something about riding on a motorcycle it just did something to you, it was so much fun. This took my mind off what's her name. When we got to her house she told me that "there were more fish in the ocean. There are plenty other nice girls, you will see, don't worry about her". Then my favorite song came on the radio Disco Duck, I jumped up and danced around the livingroom. When I got back I found out she took off all her cloths and got in the bed. That night she helped me to see that "you can't always get what you want, I said you can't always get what you want, but if you try sometimes, you'll find, you get what you need ahhh yeh Baby"! That's what Mick Jigger says. That was a night that I will never forget. I guess it's where I started my life philosophy. Never get stuck on one girl because there are more that will appreciate you. Our relationship didn't go very far she always insisted that I was too young for her. I wish it would of worked she was such a nice lady that helped me a lot. I guess I was a real inexperienced shy guy at first. I listen and wasn't very wild. I will always love what she did for me. That is the older women in my life that taught me what I know about Love and relationships. Which wasn't much.

After working all summer I quit the Ford Motor Company. I earned a lot of money because of overtime. I was working midnights at the time and because I worked all night there wasn't much time to spend my money. I learned to work many different jobs their but the work had no challenge. I still have not found the work or career that would complete me. Something that I would enjoy coming to work for, my dream job.

My birthday present to myself was a plane ticket to California the San Francisco Bay. My new dream was to dance on Soul Train. I have always thought that I was a good dancer, so what better place to go than Hollywood. After visiting here with my family my mind was blown. Brenda said she was going to California too. All I could think of was living here for the rest of my life. I lived with my aunt Jewell in Oakland because she was the first to come get me from the airport. My mother has two sisters in California one lives in San Francisco, Josie and the other in Oakland. She had four fine daughters that I used to always brag about, Cheryl, Missy, Karen and Kim. I enjoyed my trip, although I never pursued my goal. What I was interested in was Nancy. She was a beautiful fair skinned Spanish girl, she had long dark brown hair, brown eyes, and nice legs. She dressed very modestly. I was attracted to her, and she was my cousins best friend. We sat on the balcony with herb, tea, and Stevie Wonder's Songs in the key of Life, and talked all afternoon. I was still shy when it came to women but she invited me to dinner. She worked at La Piñata, a Mexican Restaurant that's where she invited me. It was close to downtown Oakland I took the bus. On the way I noticed the streets were full Beautiful women all different shapes, sizes, and colors, all wearing body suits and real skimpy thin clothing showing everything. I guess these were Streetwalkers, ladies of the night, or Hookers. I wasn't use to this because the streetwalkers in Detroit are ugly enough to scare the dogs away. I heard that prostitution is one of the oldest business known, and they had some of the best I had ever seen. I never saw so many beautiful women. They were so fine that I would have been tempted, but at the time I was so shy all I did was look. While I rode the bus I saw a sign that said Men Working over an open man hole. Someone wrote a big, WO in front of the MEN which made it read WOMEN Working. What I heard was that these women would come from all over the world to be actresses, dancers, and singers, and end up becoming whores.

When I arrived at La Piñata, Nancy was there to greet me she was working, so she directed me to my table. This was the first time I went to a Mexican restaurant, so she helped me with my order. It's wasn't long before she brought me my plate, I had fried bananas, black beans, rice and a beef enchilada. She came and sat with me and we talked, about nothing. I daydreamed about us having a relationship, and her family rejected her for talking to a black man. As I rode home I thought about her and wondered if we could ever get together. I did learn something about Mexican food, it went down easy and nice but coming out was very painful. Nothing ever became of us, but we talked and hung out together daily.

All I could think about is what a beautiful city Oakland was, and how it reminded me of Detroit but smaller. I did go on an adventure although while I was there. I heard that Iggy Pop was coming to Berkley College so I went to see the concert. David Bowie was my favorite Rock Star, I had all his records, I even met him in Detroit when he and Iggy Pop did their tour. At That time David and Iggy were more interested in the Black women. I knew plenty of girls that loved them both from school. I ran into some of them on my way to the Ponachatrain Hotel Downtown. I heard it was the Hotel they stayed at so I went to the bar a waited. A good friend grew up with me that lived on Griggs, Theresa, Debra was talking to David Bowie. Her and Dena had a table and they invited me to sit with them. I meet David that night sitting at a table with him, and ten of the most beautiful black women in Detroit. David asked me I would like a drink, I said No, and He asked me why was I in a bar if I didn't drink. One drink too many. Everyone at the table laughed, I had a very good time. As I sat at the table I saw David & Iggy take up to their room two by two everyone of them, and then some more. By the end of the night we were invited up to the room of the Drummer, we partied the night away, playing and singing, with some other members of the band and some other women I knew that weren't fine enough to be chosen.

I just had to go to the concert, although I didn't buy a ticket. Another trick I learned how to get in free at concerts. I just broke through the crowd as they were taking the tickets and got in. But this wasn't the way I learned, I was just winging it. I forgot one thing, in Berkley everyone was white, I might have been the only Black guy at the concert. Right before the end, I was right up at the front enjoying the show, the guards grabbed me and threw me out on my ass. I wondered how they found me I guess my color betrayed me.

Well time went on and I did meet a nice black tall light skin young lady. Who looked like Kim Novak the movie actress. She lived down the street from my cousin Cheryl's house. I helped them move in, she lived with her sister. I put down some carpet for them, and just hung out down at there Apartment when she was there. Time went on I had I lots of fun going between Oakland and San Francisco. I had an Aunt in San Francisco that lived in the Diamond Hills Sub, she introduced me to her best friend's son. We hung out went to a party, he showed me around. I learned to drink Tequila when I first came here. Tony had a superbad ride a Cuda with a 385 engine, and it was super fast, jumping the hills of the San Francisco Bay was great fun. San Fan is a beautiful city with streets going up and down hills, I met a lot of his friends and we went all over. We went to one party at a luxury house in the Diamond Hills, and they were playing Marvin Gaye's New record "Let's Get it on". Being new and not knowing anybody the party wasn't that fun to me. He knew everyone I knew no one and I couldn't get any of the beautiful women to pay me any attention. I didn't go to school with them so I guess I was Mr. nobody. We hung till early morning I should of stayed with my aunt in San Fan, but Oakland was more familiar. I was aunts Jewel's favorite, and she didn't have any sons. That's why she was the first to pick me up from the airport, so I stayed in Oakland.

It wasn't long before I ran out of money. I called my mother, and she told me my father had a job for me. Right before I left I got mad, and said I'm leaving. When I turned eighteen and nothing seemed to work out the way I planned. My mother told me "Don't burn your bridge". I really didn't know what she was talking about, but I'm glad I left on good terms. That made the returns trip not so bad.

When I got back my mother said "the prodigal son returns". I guess I was like the boy in the parable, I did go to a far away land. I did spend all my money, although I worked for mine. My father was happy at my return, he had me a new job. My mother was very active in our local church. When I went to California I lost my belief in God, and Christ. It was Easter and I was so used to going to Church I asked about going to one. A friend of my Aunt asked me to go his Church, what I didn't know was it was a Holiness Church. I went and I wore my suit that was hand made by my mother, it was light blue with a flowered vest. (The very same suit I was stood up for my senior prom in, bad luck suit) After the service I was approached by some of the ministers, and I told them that I was saved. They asked me if I received the Holy Ghost, I should of said yes but, I say no. I heard about the way people used to jump around like they were crazy at some churches. We didn't do that at our church we were real laid back. We were Methodist, although my old church pastor use to foam at the mouth screaming at the top of his lungs preaching about Hell. I used to visit Greater Grace Church with Junior Scott to look for pretty girls. They got real happy there jumping and hollering and running all around. I wanted nothing to do with that. I was happy with my faith, my church and Pastor Williams, and all he taught me. They told me that I was not really saved until I received the Holy Ghost. They asked me to try to receive the Holy Ghost and it would make me feel better, and I would really be saved. We argued I stood my ground and they asked me to try it and if I didn't like it I could go. They then took me in this dark basement with some red lights, in a room, and they had me get on my knees and repeat saying "I love Jesus" over and over. I was down there for a long time, two or three hours, and they wouldn't let me leave until I spoke in tongues. I was sweaty, tired, and my words started to slur together, I knew what they wanted so I faked it so I could get out of there. "SUVEE LOSDE THUDE NFMRKFJ GHYK. HLKL KFK LYLYYPYLH THEUR YTKD J GDXMNIJW,." so they said "yeh, yeh you got it, YOU GOT IT ". When they let me upstairs they asked me don't I feel better and I told them "No" and ran out the door. I was so mad that day how could my religion get me in trouble. I hear people getting in trouble with Drugs, bad women, stealing, lying, cheating but *I never knew that Jesus would get me in deep waters.* I felt that day I was taken advantaged of, it was like I was abused. This cut me deep to my heart everything I believed was now all a fake. The school told me there was no god just myths and fairy tales. In school I secretly held my beliefs to myself. I would always belief what my mother said while raising us. We heard bible verses all day, we would learn old testament verses for church and at home. I was a alter boy, in the church choir, and in many church plays. God's word was woven deep in my heart. David was my favorite hero. That day I blamed God especially Jesus, for how could he let this happen to me. I was new to the faith if God was really real, why would he let this happen to me. As a child I always felt if God was real why he couldn't just speak to us like he did in the Bible. My mother wanted to leave our old Church, because I asked too many question, and the Pastor couldn't answer them. Like if God spoke to all the Saints in the bible why can't he speak any more? All our old pastor could do was verbally create the torments we would go through if went to hell, in his sermons. Although I was back in Detroit, I was changed on the inside. Now I feel that things just happen. There was no God, although a good idea. If there is a God, he has no power, or for some reason he's not speaking any more. Once I heard that God was made—up just to make people act good. Everything I heard from the street was not that reliable.

While I was back in Detroit and I looked up some of my good friends, like Butch, Darren Martin, and some school friends to hang with. I was very happy to be back in Detroit while hanging with O, he introduced me to some of his Eastside friends. We went to the eastside to meet these fine young ladies, I was supposed to talk to Jonnie. She was fine light skinned with green eyes, but when I met her sister I fell for her right away. Sylvia looked like her sister, but was thinner and taller. We both liked each other, and had some of the same things interests like music, partying so we hung for the next three days straight. Hanging out on the Eastside with some of O's friends was the bomb meeting new friends and having fun. It was Glen the Saxophone player, Amp the Keyboardist, Toney the Model and Sylvia and Jonnie the French girls, we all had a good time. Amp would drive us around in his small Renault Le Car it would be at least five of us in at one time. We went to Northland to hang out and have fun, the mall was one of the best places to hang. This all made the time go by fast while I waited for my new job to start.

I knew my father had some job for me but I didn't ask what. We lived at that time in the University District, on Birchcrest Street by Seven mile and Livernois. We had a very nice brick house with five bedrooms, right across from Sherwood Forrest. It was a very nice neighborhood full of beautiful girls, in a well to do area. My father at the time was the Director of Public Works he worked his way up from being an accountant for the City of Detroit. Early Monday morning before he left for work he gave me a newspaper and on it was circled "HIRING DETROIT FIRE FIGHTERS". The only thing I could think of was

Smokey the Bear saying "Only you can prevent Forrest Fires". As a child I always saw the Smokey the Bears on commercials, so I thought I'd be fighting forest fires. I never went to a Detroit Fire House, I couldn't tell you where any of them are located. I don't know how I looked over this as a career choice. I know that I loved playing with fire, I was a firebug.

Chapter 3
TRAINING ACADEMY

SINCE THE DISCOVERY OF FIRE there arose men brave enough to handle these flames. These men were called shaman or firemen. Their rank in society rose because of the use of this new energy. Fire was then used not only in cooking but in warfare as an easy way to take enemies territories by burning them down. Because fire could consume a whole city with in hours, fire fighting became a profession. Early in the Roman empire when one home would catch on fire, a fire company would arrive a quote the cost before entering the fire. The first fire departments in America were volunteer services, the station housed all the equipment. When the fire bell rang everyone would stop their work, leave their jobs and go fight the fire. The Detroit fire department is one of the best in the country.

These were all the thoughts I had when it came to me joining the Detroit Fire Department. I was very happy to become a fire fighter. The requirements were High School Diploma, or GED, over 18 years of age, be a Detroit resident. My life was totally enriched by my home scientist training, or fire bug training with live experiments. I'd find out if, I WAS BRAVE, A COWARD, OR CRAZY, WHILE MOST PEOPLE WILL BE RUNNING OUT I WOULD BE RUNNING IN TO BATTLE A BLAZING FIRE.

First I turned in the application in at the address that was on the newspaper my father gave me. It was at the Super Truck 7, firehouse on Lafayette and Mount Elliot. There was a long line of applicants Black and White, men and women. I guess this was a good paying job, so lots of people came. This was a time of high unemployment and the opening of this job was big. In this line was one of every nationality, race and religion. Irish, Polish, Italian, Muslim, Jehovah Witness, southern blacks, northern blacks, from as far as Texas to Colorado and as close as Chicago and Cleveland they all came for a good paying dangerous job. I waited in line when it was my turn I turned in the application. They gave us a sheet with more information on it. It told the base pay which was $14,000. a year, and we would be paid to go through training for six months. It would be two more test to go, a written one, and a physical test. Just graduating from High School I knew that I was ready for both of them. I took the written test first, if you passed it you would go on to the next. That test was so simple, I heard later that it was made easy so more Blacks could be hired. I don't know if that's the truth, but I do know that when Mayor Coleman Young got in office in 1972, he said he'd make the Police and Fire Departments both fifty percent Black. At this time there were more Blacks living in Detroit than ever, but the Police and Fire Departments were both more than ninety percent White.

In the mail I got a notice that I passed the written test, and was scheduled for the Physical Agility Test. I did some running to prepare, in fact since I ran track in High School from 1973 to 1975. I already would run at least one to five mile per day early in the morning. I went to the State Track Meet, and ran in two events, 440 relay, and the mile relay. My high School won the Mile Relay, and the 440 relay race. I did some weight lifting, push ups to prepare myself. The Test was at the Detroit Training Academy, on Warren and Lawton, I caught the bus, it wasn't hard to find.

I saw about fifty people there to take the test, Black, White, and women too. There were about six or seven different Test instructors giving the test. The Stair Test consisted of a bundle of line and ten flights of stairs, we would put the bundle on our shoulders and run up the stairs, and back down while they timed us. The Ladder Test was a ladder on the wall we would have to take it off the wall stand it up then put it back on the wall. The Roof Simulation Test had buckets filled that weighed about twenty five pounds each and, we would have to walk across a simulated roof with the buckets in our hands, across, and back all while being timed. This is what they used to pick who would be the new trainees for the fire academy.

I waited to see if I was chosen, for the job. I was thinking If I don't get this what will I do. One day I was walking over Butch's house, he live on the other side of Livernois, and I ran into a Beautiful Young Lady, honey brown, with a big Angela Davis natural. She was about 5'5" with a very shapely figure, and she was super fine. I approached her with a regular rap like what's your name, She said her name was Ramona. I had a natural also, and was in the best shape of my life, and maybe she felt the same way about me. It was said at the time that I had a the body of Adonis, some Greek god or something. At the time I was 6'2" chocolate brown, with light brown eyes, a big wide chess big thick thighs that you could see my muscles flex when I walked. (That's what some young lady told me at summer camp) That's what playing football from sunup till dawn, or running 5 to 10 miles a day, will make a man look like. I was always thin but lately I started to thicken up. Some said that I was cute, not fine, just cute, with a big bright smile. It was like we were a match made in heaven. We went everywhere together, and when we were together heads turned, cause she was a brick house. Just to see her in a tank top and those torn blue jean shorts, car horns would blow, and almost have an accident when she walked down the street.

Her father was a Detroit Police officer and his best friend was a Fireman. The days we spent made time go by faster, it seamed as if we were meant to be together for life. The next thing I knew the letter came and I made it. I was to start the academy right before my 19th birthday. Now I was on my way to become the youngest black fire fighter in the city of Detroit. It was about a week before I was to start the academy I was leaving Darren's house, and on my way to Ramona's house. I was driving my Honda Chopper motorcycle, down Curtis, and I came up to a light at Roselawn in front of Bagley elementary school , there was a car pulling up, so I slowed down. It looked like she stopped , so I hit the throttle because I had the green light. Soon as I took off she did also. My bike hit the side of her car door, and flew over the hood of the car. I could see her as see watch me flying over the car as I hit the ground. I hit my knee hard when I came down. I must of flew at lease 15 feet in the air,(I always record my flight time and I always enjoy a flight) and slid another 10 feet. I wore a helmet although I didn't hit my head, just my knees were hurt. Someone called the EMS and they took me to the Hospital,

My mother and my girlfriend came to the Hospital to see me, I asked my mother about my bike. She told me they called Mr. Moore went to get it but it was gone when he arrived. Mr. Moore was a neighbor from Griggs street he was the man that used to fly up and down the street burning rubber. He was from the Kentucky Hills a old-timer moonshine run man, he had a chicken coop in his backyard. His rooster would wake us up every morning, and he had a garden with corn, greens, everything. He would help everyone in the neighborhood like the Father of the street. He helped my father many times. He was a very big man with curly black hair he looked like a light shinned, Dizzy Gillespie, and he talked cool talk too. It was like he was scatting while he talked, he called me Dwayanie-Mo, he gave everybody nick-names. He worked at a car shop around the corner and always drove a Cadillac.

I was just glad I was still alive. I had the best family anyone could ask for, a beautiful girlfriend, and a new job, and everything to live for. This was the day my angel kicked in, the way he lifted me off my bike and flew me to safety, this would be the beginning of many more fantastic miracles in the saving of my life. If I had of hit the car with that force I could have been injured for life, and if I couldn't pass the physical I would of never got hired. This wasn't the first time that I thought I might be crippled or killed, and something would happen to change the outcome.

We had to take a Physical before we were sent to the academy, it was just like joining the armed forces. We were all lined up and they checked us out all that made it so far. Then I was send to the Academy for my first day of class. The academy was in a firehouse they had classrooms upstairs, it was the same place I took the Physical Agility

Test. I was prepared for a full days work, then I was pulled out of class, they sent me back to the Medical Division, Downtown. When I got down there they told me that I had a ill-regular heart beat, and that I fail the physical. I remember taking a physical for the football team at Mumford, and the Doctors were puzzled about the sound of my heart. The examining Doctor called the other Doctor to here my heart, but the other Doctor said that their was no problem. The Fire Department Doctor said I had an ill regular heart beat. (My Rock and Roll heart) They said that this was signs of heart problems, and that I was out of the running. (all the people that tried to join I guess that had to find a way to get rid of some of them) I went home sad, and for the next few days I felt as if I did have heart problems. I thought that I would die soon, and just sat around the house sad, and confused. My father set me up with a heart specialist, that costs two hundred dollars, that was a lot of money then. My father was very tight on money this was monumental. After coming back from that, my mother drove me there, they found no signs of heart problems. A Heart specialists said that my heart just beats different, and that I have an athletic heart. It take a lot of energy to get my heart pumping fast, because of all my sports activities. I guess all those days of playing football from sun up till dawn paid off. My father set it up with the Medical Department I had to bring the finding there, and they put me back in class. I had to start the next class because I was too far behind in that one. My father to the rescue again, with out him I would have went on thinking that I had heart problems for the rest of my life. I learned if you want to do something, don't give up so easy.

Now it was time for me to start the Academy for the second time. When I was refused and turned away from something I want, when I get it, I work a lot harder. I was determined to get this done no matter what, ready this time to be the best I could be. The day I started at the academy I came on time, we were in the classroom upstairs and this time I wasn't pulled out. My class was about 50/50 Black and White, with five women. These will be the first women ever to become fire fighters, if they pasted the training. It was about thirty-five or forty people in the class, and they took us though all the fire fighting procedures. Ventilation was the way study of air flow, after the fire was out we had different way to push the smoke and heat out. Forcible Entry how enter in a property that was locked Commercial and residential homes. They taught us different ways we could enter a structure with devices that prevented entrance like, security systems, locks, gates, doors, windows, and even concrete and brick walls. Fire science was how fire burned, Fuel + Oxygen + Spark = Fire, All these elements were needed to keep the combustion alive. The study of flammable liquids where they are stored and how to battle them. Engine Maneuvers was all the different ways to set up of lines, fire fighting nozzles, and pumping engines. Ladder Maneuvers was about setting up ladders, going on roofs, opening them up for ventilation, setting up water towers. Tools of the trade was the study of all firefighting tools what they used and how to use them. Prompier Training was on how to scale large buildings, from the outside, how to slide down ropes, and firefighting maneuvers on large buildings. We were also taught the Administration system of the Fire Department and how seniority system works. We had to learn how to tie 20 different knots on equipment and to do different functions. Most of this knowledge came from the Navy, merchant marines and the boy scouts.

Then we had to march and run later in the afternoon, and they taught us military style marches, and lining up techniques as well as having us run a mile and a half every day. After the class room studies they took us out and asked if anyone had military experiences, then they used them to line up the class and march around the back lot. That's when we found out who was from the armed forces that was in our class. That's when I learned about Big Brock, he was from the U.S. Navy, a big three hundred and fifty pound light skinned black man. He became the back bone of our Academy class, the second class of "77". He was big strong and knowledgeable of fire fighting procedures, in the navy you had to know about putting out fires, all about hoses, line and nozzles. He lined us up and marched us around the back lot, and after that everyone looked up to him, because most of us were learning things we never knew. They used different classmates to do the line up and march, I guess to see who had experience. Well one day another it was another classmate turn and it was Abdullah and he was a Muslim he had some training in military marching also. When he was in charge he lined us up, and when he hollered out "Atteee-Huuuuut, Dreeess—right—dress—Looking Gooood" in a very high pitched voice, in a foreign sing songy kind of way. There was a little laughing in the ranks, you see his accent was a little different. He learned his training with the Muslims, I found out latter that his father was very high up in the Islam religion in Detroit. Not only him but all most everyone in that class parents had important places with the City. Bruce's father was the President in charge of the Fire Fighting Union. We had a lot of sons of important City officials, in fact my father was in charge of Detroit Public Works. In the past Fire Fighting was a family trade, if your father was one then you would be one. Fire fighters not only fought fires but they had construction skills, they did roofing, fire repairs, brick work, plumbing, and most firemen were white. They were Italian, Polish, Irish, Hillbillies, and any tough strong Americans, but not many blacks, and they wanted to keep it that way. Mayor Coleman Young was changing a tradition with this new group of employees, not only blacks but women also.

I would have six months in the Fire Academy, and then six months in a Fire House, if I pasted them both then I would become a Fire Fighter. They broke us up into groups of six and we would do the fire fighting techniques together, and it was a competition between us. One that would let us know was a trainee named French, he was black, and he would come to our group laughing and talking about how we weren't doing it right. He was a light brown tall young man who thought he was gods gift to the world. Let him tell it he was a pro football player taking a break from college and Hot rod racing. He had a big mouth always talking about someone and bragging on himself, about how good he and his group was. He was always sticking his head through from another side of a room saying something like the smart ass he was.

My team was the best in my eyes, we had some good people on it. We had Big Brock who knew a lot about the training because of his past. There was Lester he was a older black man from the Air Force, he worn glasses brown skinned and had a curly short natural, and was very intelligent. I another guy I liked was DeMicheal a white young man about thirty eight, tall with always a good sence of humor a real nice person. We had a women in our group she was small and, it seemed as if she was only here for the pay, but she tried hard. Then it was Bruce a young white man who knew everything about fire fighting, because his father was one, and his family had a long line of fire fighters. He was always playing and he didn't care about anything. I remember when they first let us hold the hose and shoot water, he started to wet people with it. He shoot water in the front of the building wetting people that walked by, he was always doing something crazy. I was reserved and always ready to learn, I didn't brag, but loved doing the dangerous exercises, especially the ones with height included. Big Brock and Lester were the leaders, Bruce and I were the youth, and DeMicheal always put a positive light to it, and the girls were scared. We got through all our exercises in record time, and we were either the first or second group that did the best. I was very dedicated because I loved everything about fire fighting. One day while we had a lunch I would stay in the classroom studying and would always bring a lunch. The Commissioner of the Fire Department came in and sat down with me and talked to me. He asked how I liked it and why I wasn't out to lunch with everyone else, I just told him how I liked it and that I was just studying. I found out later what was going on at lunch, some were drinking beer, some were smoking weed, but I stayed to myself and wasn't about to get in any trouble. I didn't know that my father and the Commissioner were good friends until my mother told me later. They were both appointees I guess I should of known, but I never went to my fathers office, so I never knew. All I knew was that I found out what I wanted to be in life, and nothing was going to stop me. I enjoyed everything about the training, and the Officers in charge I looked up to them for all I learned.

My Instructors at the academy were Lt. Robinson, Lt. Lauer, Captain Towne, Lt. Garrison, they were the main ones teaching us our new duties. Captain Towne a older white gentleman taught the engine operations, hose, pipe, and pumping hook-ups in the class room. Lt. Robinson a heavy set older black man that always had a smile taught Fire Science in the classroom. Lt. Lauer was white, and Lt. Garrison was black both younger men in very good shape taught the exercises on the net, climbing walls, putting up ladders, on roofs, in the smoke house, extending line up flights of stairs, operating the hoses, and most of the dangerous work. During the exercises Lt Lauer would always call on me to answer question and demonstrate new procedures. I don't know if he just knew my name or if he knew of my father on why he would always call for me but I was always ready. He was a real smart-alecky, and was always proving something and making us look like fools if he could. Others would run and hide when they saw him because they knew he would call on them to do something hard. Although I never did, I wasn't afraid of him in fact I liked him a lot. I knew that he knew his business, and I wanted to learn everything he had to teach.

What did I learn, although it took many years for me to realize what I learned was what I was looking for all my life. First I learned the secret of fire, the total break down of the chemistry flammables liquids. How they burn, how you can trace them, what color of the smoke can tell you about what is burning. That it is the fumes that burn, the gas from the liquids that burns not the liquid itself. How when plastic burns it gives off a smoke that could kill you. How when fire burns it makes a gas called carbon dioxide, that is a deadly gas that kills, and causes brain damage. That smoke taken in through the lungs causes irreversible permanent lung damage, and once you reach a certain point you just die. How smoke first seduces you with a dream like state, while killing you slowly, if you don't wake up in time. Smoke rises, while air is right on the floor, if you stand up you can die, if you crawl on the floor you can get out of a burning house. Stop—Drop and Roll what we teach to all school kids, running with fire will increase the flames, Dropping and Rolling can put them out. To anyone else all this would sound scary , but to me I was intrigued. They really told us straight what we were in for, you can die, this is a very dangerous business. There was a part of me that thought could I really do this, was I brave, how was all this suppose to work? I think they tried to scare us on purpose, because they wanted you to except the risk, and not think of it, and do the best job that you could.

Heights was my second love, I wanted to fly, but if I couldn't I'll be happy on the top of the roof, or the top of a water tower. They taught us how the scale a high rise building from the outside, floor by floor. We used this great big hook that would grab the next floor and then you would climb up it to the next floor. This was as high as I could get, and I enjoyed all the exercises. It was Lt Lauer that taught how to get up on the safety net, and it was him that taught us to scale ten floors in the air, then lean back held by our partner. My partner was a black young lady, about five foot five, 125 pounds, and very scared, but I gave her props, because she did it. At the time I didn't know she was scared because she never said anything about it. That day as I leaned out that top of the tenth floor, over the net, I could smell her sweat, and It was a very strong womanly smell. I knew because we worked closely together that she was scared as hell. It took me a long time to realizes that what I was doing I wanted to, but what she was doing she didn't want to she just wanted a good paying job. For her to go this far for a job was something, me I lived my whole life just for this. All I could think was that she had more heart than me to do this to take care of her family was real big.

To past this course and go to the firehouse we had to do the physical requirement, past the final physical agility test, and run a mile and a half under five minutes. All the teams were practicing fifty push-ups, deep knee bends, climb ten flights of stairs with an oxygen tank on your back, and twenty pounds of line in your arms, and ten pull-ups. The women were having a hard time with the push-ups, and the pull-up, and the officers were trying to help them. The first time Big Brock tried the pull-ups, he could only do one as we went on he did more. Now he was at lease three hundred and fifty pounds easy, that was a lot of weight, at about six feet tall. While the weeks passed by Big Brock started doing more and more, he went from three, to five, but the time was getting shorter. Sergeant Lauer made fun of Big Brock because he couldn't do the pull-ups " I thought you were tough". The whole academy was behind him, he became the heart behind all of us. The Question on all of our minds was who was going to make it. We found our that Coleman Young's niece was in our class, and she was something else. She was very proud, and outspoken, a lot of our class didn't like her. She was very good looking, light skinned, about five feet six, with a very nice shape. Yes I was interested, but I wasn't in her group, I guess if my uncle was the Mayor, I'd be a little high and mighty too. Some of the women were getting close, but not the one in our group. She couldn't do the Push-ups or the pull-ups. Big Brock got closer but was still a little off, only doing eight. The whole academy would cheered him on as he would battle that bar, he wasn't going to let that bar stop him. I was watching a real Hero Big Brock was the man. I found out he live by me, and he started to picking me up, because I was catching the bus before that. Lester the Air Force guy would ride with us, I sat in the back. They both had a lot in common, both were married, both served in the Vietnam War. They would talk about the service, Brock was the strength, and Lester was the brains, and I just listen, and learned, together they had a wealth of experience. DeMicheal would keep us laughing and in good spirit. I had everything under control, being in the best shape of my life. The Doctor said that I have a athletic heart, and it took a lot to get it running fast. That means while others hearts are pumping fast, mine was just getting started. I did have one problem the accident, after flying over the car I came down on my knee. I never told anyone about it, and I was hiding it. When we did deep knee bents, I could just drop to the ground and push back up with one knee. I had to get past this test without them finding out.

I ate, slept, and drank the Detroit Fire Department, I took copious notes, and studied late in the nights. I was late twice on account of I was catching the bus before Brock started to pick us up along the way. That could have been why Lt. Lauer was always on my case.

They tried to scare us with the Smoke House. It was a little house on the lot in the back of the academy. It was first French telling us they couldn't make it through , and on how hard it was going to be. We would have to go all the way through and come out on the other side to pass. They said a lot of people didn't make it, because you couldn't wear a mask you had to go with out one. I admit I was scare of this, and this was my first real test. This house was filled with smoke, then they send you through one at a time. When I first got in it, you couldn't see a thing, I had to feel with my hands, it was like a rat maze, it turned from one side to another. I came to the end of a wall and was stuck in a room, it took me a little while, but I found the opening high in the air, so I crawled out of that room now up higher it was full of smoke, I was out of air. Coughing and choking I kept going on, I just used my fingers as eyes, feeling around until I found my way out. Then it seemed as if I dropped out of the crawl space to hit the ground again, but it was good cause the air at the bottom had more oxygen. Now it was still pitch black, I couldn't even see my hand right in front of me, but the rest was easy as I followed the maze to the outside. That was the scariest thing I ever done, and I was proud of myself, because I didn't know if I was going to make it. That was the first clue that I might be brave, because I didn't give up, and I think that's what they were looking for. We heard some people got stuck and cried for help and the offices rushed in to get them out. This was a dangerous exercise that could of killed someone, and not many fire academies had smoke houses.

After the smokehouse they had a movie for us to watch, about a train accident. We went to the classroom to watch it, the training was almost over we took all our test and this was part of the last stages. The scene was set somewhere in America on a railroad track. A train derailment had happen and the fire department was sent out, along with a camera crew. The train was laying on the side of the track all the cars were on their side. The movie showed the train and the fire dapartment veichiles respond to the emergency. They pulled up and started to pull out their equipment, the ladder truck set up a water tower. On that train was a flammable liquid in a storage rail car, and it was laying on its side. We saw them set up line hoses, and all kinds of equipment, then the camera started to shake and fell to the ground. The screen went black and a subtitle came on the screen and it was written EVERYONE THAT RESPONDED TO THAT ALARM IS NOW DEAD.

When the temperature in the tanker reaches a certain degree it will explode. The movie went off and that was it. I don't know how everyone else felt, but I had a serious understanding of this job. After all I went through do I still have a choice. Many jobs are not available to black men with just a high school education, so I better not mess this one up. This was a reality on how dangerous this job really is, and that I could be killed at anytime. There was a lot of talk, and I don't know who changed their mind on going further with this career. Death was something that I didn't know much about, but I felt like I wouldn't die anytime soon. I stored this in my head, and just thought it wasn't going to be me.

Our final examine was coming up, and we had a group of the black trainees who came together for a study session. One of our instructors was their, and they went over everything that was going to be on the test. We all met at Norris Frye's Apartment, he was a cool black young gentleman, with his head on straight. In my book he was a player and a ladies man, smart and connected. I don't know how they put this all together, but he had some help.

I don't know if all the white trainees got together for a study session. That evening we went over all the text for the final, this was knew for a lot of all. I went with Lester and Brock, when we got there we saw that Frye was getting cool with one of the ladies in the class. Most of the Black female trainees were there, everybody was there for business. We stayed late and I got to meet and talk with a lot of the other trainees. When we were at the Academy we never had time to get to know each other.

On Monday we took our test, and it was long and hard. Having a young mind, I did pretty good then we did our physical test. That was easy for me, all I had to do was not to let them find out that my knee was hurt. The test took out a lot of trainees most of the women, and a lot of the men too. After that movie I felt some didn't want to pass.

I was happy just to get paid for the training. Now for all the ones left we had to run the mile and a half under five minutes. They told us that they were going to give the fastest runner a trophie, and I wanted it. I trained all week for this run, I was a sprinter so this wasn't my race. We were going to do the run at the Wayne State College campus track. I showed up like just another track meet. I was ready to do my best. I did my stretches and limbered up, then I did a couple of sprints to get ready. We all lined up on the track outside the football field, when the gun went off I took off. Everyone knew that I was a good runner, I had a good form and a good pace. I started in the lead I set the pace not to fast but I had a good stretch, I lead the pack for about three to four laps. It was a quarter mile track so we had to do six laps to make a mile and a half. At about the top of the fourth lap going to the fifth, someone came up behind me and tried to pass me. I increased my speed so he couldn't , then at the bottom of the lap at the curve he jumped on the inside of the lane and pushed me out. When a lead man is running the proper way to past is on the outside, because the leader has used his energy to lead, it takes more strengthen to pass on the outside. When he took the inside lane on a curve I was pushed to the outside lane, that means I'm running more distance. I fought for the lead, but it was taking to much energy so I let him have the lead. It was the last lap he was in the lead, it was Poole. I jumped on his tail and stayed there it was just him and I and we lead the pack by half the track. I saved my power and stayed as close as I could behind him. If we had of kept on fighting for the lead no telling what would of happen. I was upset that he came on the inside to take the lead. He might not have ran track in school to know what he did was wrong, but I didn't say a word. I just trailed him all the way through the last lap. When we got to the last curve I was still trailing by just a few steps. When we came out of that last turn and went into the last stretch at the straight away, I hit it. We fanned out and went side by side battling for the lead. Being a sprinter my coach always told us to save enough power for the last of the race, and I did. This was not my race and I was very tired, but I didn't care. Now it was my turn, he thought that I lost, but I put it in third gear and I turned it on. I went by him so fast he didn't know what was happening. Maybe he was tired and he thought it was over. The finish line was right in front of me, I kicked my knees up so high, and pushed with all I had. My track coach would have been proud of me that day, all he taught me paid off. I won the race, and that was one of the proudest day in my life. My classmates jumped with joy and shouted out , they couldn't believe it. They though I had lost, but I came from behind to get it at the end. I guess I had fans that I didn't know about. Poole was a little older than me probably twenty five, to my nineteen, and he looked like a experience runner. I think I only got him by surprise, because he thought that after fighting for the lead, I didn't have enough power to take it back. He might have been a long distance man but I was a sprinter, that was my edge. Although I was annoyed I never spoke to him about how he took the lead. I set a all time records for the fastest mile and a half ever, without his help I would of never ran that race that fast. He was a good

friend, and we never had bad words toward each other, he congratulated me also.

We had a physical at the medical department then the Graduation after that we would be assigned to a Fire Station. I got my test final back and I graduated with a 93%, the physical test were just pass or fail, and I passed them all. We were still at the training Academy working on our Graduation exercise. The instructors were a lot more informal, welcoming us in the fold. Lt Robinson met me in the hallway and said, I was suppose to be helping you, he smiled and with a chuckle he said "but you didn't need any help." For the graduation ceremony part of our team was selected to scale the wall, others were to slide down a rope. At the graduation I was feeling very proud, I have finally completed something, it was one of my happiest days in my life. Maybe I couldn't fly planes, but I could fly high at the Detroit Fire Department.

Although it is told to us at a very early age, that we can be anything we wanted. I found out that with a lot of work, a lot of praying, and a lot of getting up again, you may get what you want. I have now found something I'm happy with, and all because my father knew me. Upstairs back in classroom they were now telling us our fire stations we were assigned. Mine was Engine 49, it was located at Grand River and Manor, the west side, not that far from where we lived. I was told that it was a very good station, and that it was a very fast station. The more fires you have the better you learn and, the quicker, and I was at the fastest. My mother came and my girlfriend Ramona, I heard my father was here, and that was strange because this was the first event my father showed up for. The Graduation begain and I did the exercise where we climbed up to the tenth floor from the outside. As I hung out the tenth floor my mother a beautiful light skinned woman, with long light brown hair and green eyes, saw me and said

"He's made it, he's flying. The prodical son returns, kill the fatted calf and put a ring on his finger, Lord I strech my hands out to thy, for I no other help I know." My mother was very proud of me passing the course.

We were all sat down in front of the podium on the back lot of the Fire Academy. On the podium sat the Detroit dignitaries and I heard from a classmate that my father was sitting up there with them. I looked up and there was Mayor Coleman Young, next to him was Commisioner Melvin Jefferson, and next to him was my father. At that time I didn't think he was an Apointee, but he was in the budget department. When I walked up to the stage, I was first because my last name was Abrams, there was my father to shake my hand and the Fire Department Commissioner Melvin Jefferson, Mayor Coleman Young, Fire Marshall, the Chief of the Academy, and City Officials. I was presented a trophy for the fastest ran mile and a half, for the Detroit Fire Academy Class of 1977.

I looked around and it seemed as if everyone made it, but their were a few that didn't make it. The Mayor's neice, and that girl in my group, some might have been glad, and some scared, because none of us knew what was in store for us next. My girlfriend Ramona was there and she was looking very good, she had a very pretty dress on. I was in love, it seemed as if I had everthing I wanted. We make love that night like nothing else, cause she had everything I needed , and more. I should have married her right then, but I had six months of being a Trial Fire Fighter before I became hired as a fire fighter if I passed. To have a wife you need a life, and I had to pass my probation period before I was sure. Any excuse, the truth was I was scared of commitment and marriage.

My father send me out with my brother to find a car, my first car. We went to the Ford dealer on Woodward, and I picked out a Blue Ford Econoline Van. Then I went to Art Van and bought a pit sectional to go inside, with some more custom work from a Van shop.

When I was in Oakland I rode in Eric Grahams customized van he was Larry Grahams younger brother, my cousin was Missy was married to him. She used to make the costumes for the group Grahams Central station. After riding in one now I wanted a custom van, so I built one myself. Ramona and I got caught one late night, getting busy in my parents station wagon by some rent-a-cop. Now I wanted a ride with a little more privacy, and now I got one.

My girl friend Ramona got real sick, I found out later she had a miscarriage. If I would of known she was pregnant I would of asked her to marry me. If she had that baby we would be still married today. Well that didn't help our relationship. I was more interested in how I was going to do at this new Fire House. I heard it was a fast house and that was suppose to be good for me. They said it as if they were doing me a favor, I don't know if I felt the way they did. I rode around in my new van and looked at the area, then I went in and introduced myself to the crew of Engine 49. It was a single engine house. Being by itself, they would respond to all fires in the area as a first engine or a back-up engine.

Chapter 4
ENGINE 49

MY FIRST STATION WILL BE Engine 49. It's location is Grand River at Meyers, this was supposed to be a very fast engine house. Which means a lot of fires, although it's not where I wanted to go. I wanted to work at Engine 51, which was at Livernois and Curtis. By the way, it would have been perfect. It was close to my house, we lived at Birchcrest and Curtis, three blocks away.

My first lesson in working for the city was having a seniority system, that makes everything different. Engine 51 was one of the most highly sought after stations because of it's location, and being new to the department, the best I could do was to visit it. I walked there one day and met the fire fighters, at the time a famous Black fire fighter called "Action Jackson" ran there. He was a big brown heavy set man very muscular about 5' 10" weighing 250, bench press 350 or more that worked there. He was the biggest bravest bragger but the things he claimed I was impressed. His fire stories excited me and made me ready to start my new career. He felt that he was the biggest baddest strongest black man I'd ever seen and I was believing him. Move over John Henry a new hero's in town.

All the Fire Stations were rated by the workers, high for good neighborhoods, and low for bad areas with high crime activity. Now because of the new Mayor, we have stations that that have more Blacks working there than Whites. There are stations that have more Whites working there than Blacks. They have all white crews and some all black crews. Each station is known for what they are fast, slow, popular, hated, fighting, and stranded stations. The very busy houses were loved by firemen that loved fighting fires are called Fast stations. Some of them are known for playing cards, drinking, smoking, sleeping all night, weight lifting, and other activities. At the time I wanted a slower company because I wasn't sure of what I could do. I asked myself if was brave, although I learned this whole new world of firefighting, the question to myself was could I perform when called upon. I was ready to give it all I got, but could I do the job? Will I remember everything I was taught or will I freeze at the wrong time right in the middle of a fire or saving someone?

I visited my new station, it was a single engine house, right next to a strip of store fronts. A hardware store on the corner on one side, and a beer and wine store with some storefronts shops on other side. Across the street was the Toro's Motorcycle Club. (I found out later that Big Brock was a member of the Toro's) The station sat a little back between the store fronts, with a American flag flowing right over the name on the front over the bay doors ENGINE 49. I drove around the area just looking around. I remembered some of the streets and there location. I had a few days before I was to report for duty. I spent some time with Ramona, she was very happy for me, she's got a new job now working at Fairlane Mall's Gantos, a high class women clothing store. I didn't spend the time I should of with her. I paid more attention to my new job, and we only got together when we had time. Which was anytime I had a day off, and when she wasn't at work or with her girlfriends. We made love in some strange places, mostly in my parents station wagon at parks, in a secluded parking lot, a park and Drive-Ins. We loved drive-ins the whole culture of family outings. One day we woke up in the morning we just sat up and watched the sun coming up, it was beautiful. I knew I loved her, but I still didn't know much about Love. One day Ramona came by the Engine house while I was working and asked me for some money. After I gave her $50 and she called me the cheapest motherfucker she ever knew. Then she gave me hints that she been seeing someone else, at this nightclub at Fairlane. A rich Arab prince was very interested in her, she told me, but I guess I was so use to getting dumped I blew her off. I should of protested and that's what I think she wanted but I didn't. One day not to long after that her girlfriend came to see me, she was having problems with her boyfriend. We talked and hung out at my house we used to go to school together. I remembered her in school, because she was so light skinned that many people thought she was white. She was beautiful and still is the finest lady around, she reminded me of the actress Ms Lonnetta McGee in Sparkle. Lady Diana was the most beautiful young lady, tall medium built with long light brown hair, her brother was a classmate of mine. Her brother Bobby and I were friends in High School one of Darren's boys. I don't know why she came to see me but I didn't care, she talked about the problems she was having and the abuse that she was going through. I knew she was my girl best friend but I didn't care, because she was drop dead gorgeous I would of taken her in the drop of a hat. She was a very nice girl, very well behaved she told me about what Ramona was doing, but all I could think of was her. Her boyfriend was physically abusing her, and she didn't know what to do. When she left she gave me a very long kiss in the doorway. I knew that I should of stopped her but she was so fine I couldn't. Nothing ever became of it but we stayed very good friends. I knew that was the end of me and Ramona. Maybe she was testing me for Ramona but I didn't care it was worth it. I never forgot her from school. I never had a chance with her and I knew it, but I used to see her at Farmer Jacks when I went shopping for the Fire station.

At this time my job came first and all I cared about was completing my trail period and getting my badge.

I was very excited with this new job and this new Fire Station. I couldn't wait to get started, when I visited the station I met the men on the first unit. I worked on the second unit. The Fire department divides it's work days into two units, and they ran consecutively. Set up to make sure no one would work over 24 hours consecutively. Our schedule would run one day on, the next off, the next day on, then three days off. We would work eight days per week doing twenty four hour days, two days per week. This type of working schedule can make time run fast. My first working day finally came up I had to be at work 0730 hours to relieve the first unit, I was on the second unit. The day really starts at 0800 hours, but they used a thirty minute early relief period. I arrived on time I had my work uniform on just the classic blue work uniform like the police officers. I came in the side door and everyone was in the kitchen at the table drinking coffee. The first and second unit would have coffee together and talk about their day, the fires, and what happen the day before, the engine company, and what took place in the fires they had, and what they did. The fire stories would help not only the new TFF but the other fire fighters with info about buildings, hazards, and the condition they left previous fires. This is the best time to get to know each other, cause it happens every morning 0700 to 0730. When I reported in I went though the apparatus room to the office, in the dining room both officers were sitting and talking. I introduced myself and Lieutenant Krolick let me know he was my commanding officer. He asked me if I was a militant like Malcolm X, I had no idea what he was talking about. He was a older white man about fifty heavy set about 300lbs , he was a cross between WC Fields and Archie Bunker. He told me that he was a Polack and people might say behind his back that he was a dumb Polack. Then he gave me the famous speech "forget everything you learned in the Academy and learn what we have to teach you, pay strict attention to what I tell you. "When we have a fire do what I tell you, when the fires over and we get back to the station we sit down and talk about the fire". This is how we learn about fires we tell the fires stories, on what happen and we learn from them. In the morning when we change shifts, we have coffee and communicate with the other unit. That's when we tell them what happen yesterday, how the rig is running and the problems of some dangerous building, and what to be careful of. By the way I didn't drink coffee. I was just nineteen and this was a whole new world to me. I did notice that their wasn't many blacks in authority here. Many times I was the only one there, but that was cool. I've been in this situation before color, race, nationality are just more chances I will learn new and better experiences. I wasn't that good in history, what is a Polack? It was a good thing that Krolik was a teacher because he taught me everything. All from the book " the fire fighting manual". He was a from the book leader, everything was by the book. He went from A to Z in fire fighting. Many firemen thought that he was too much, and he had the reputation always doing it right. He was so much like my father. He taught me things that I would of never known. At the time I didn't know what was going on, but I learned later that he wasn't ready for a black TFF. He was hoping for someone else, maybe Berry since his father was the President of the Union and he was white. They got me, my father was an appointee to the Mayor now running the DPW, but I was black.

At the beginning, he was ready to give his firefighting experience to someone of his choice, and I wasn't it. I found out later that I messed up their all White day. You see their was a war going on in the fire department and the police department. The lines were already set up black against the white; it started with Mayor Coleman Young, when he vowed to make the department half and half. Now Detroit residents was more then 75% black, and the fire department was 95% white before him. Most of the officers were white, because of the seniority, only the appointees were black, not many black officers. Some stations had the pleasure of being all white companies, and it was a lot of things happen they wanted no one to know about. I saw a lot in those first days that I'm sure nobody wants me to tell. The way they worked with blacks living in this area, from the little boys visiting to the working girls on the street, many things were going on that they didn't want no one to know about. I won't tell I promise.

Since 1972 the Mayor has been pushing these colored folk down their throat, and they've tried to resist the advancement of these people. It started with Black Bottom, then it went to Paradise Valley, when black folks started to own more property, and businesses. When the City tax came, a lot of people with money started to move out of Detroit. After the 1967 Riot white flight was at it's highest level know by the city. The Realtors had a lot to do with this, they would call home owners and tell them that colored people are moving in their neighborhood and their property value would drop. This is how the Suburbs grew so quick and so strong. While it left Detroit in a mess, there were so many vacant homes that people just left, and they were being burned at a alarming high rate, for fun and for profit. The Fire Station I got was a bad neighborhood, that received the one of the highest fire alarm services that year. Now for some being at a fast house is good, but I was to find out that I had the worst of both worlds. This area was still had both black and white people living together and businesses still surviving. From the first working day, Lt Krolik put me to work, he took me all around whole fire station and told me my duties, the every day clean up, and special projects. First I would clean up the washroom, then the locker room, the dormitory and the restrooms. After I'd clean the upstairs now the first floor, sweep the stairway and mop it. On the main floor, the restroom, the office the dining room and the kitchen all need sweeping and mopping. This was done at all fire stations daily, the new shift would clean the whole house in the morning and be finished by 1000 hours. Special projects would be done from then till lunch or till evening , like wash windows, or polish all the brass, or dirty greasy kitchen fans, dark damp basements, dusty bell towers, wet webbed mildew hose towers, and old antique artifacts, in the attic. It all depends on the boss in charge, some would have you work till lunch, and some till evening, but not Lt Krolik I would work until finished, even if I would have to come back next week and finish. The boss was just like my father, it was like they made some backroom deal, and my father was paying off him to teach me his way. That was the reason that I didn't like him because he was my father.

Usually at fast stations less house work would be done because they would be busy fighting fires. I would work at the station, then go fight fires, when we came back I would finish my work, I'm not complaining I would never do that not verbally this is how they ran it for years, I have no problems with tradition. When it comes to fire runs I am to be on the rig when duty calls, I must drop everything and get on the rig quickly. One thing that will not be tolerated was to miss the engine on a run, or to give up the pipe before the fires out, and to be here every morning I work at 0730 hours. I am to have all my firefighting equipment ready and in working condition. It is up to me to make sure that my air tank is full at the beginning of the day, and to always be ready for the next fire. After we arrive at the fire I am to go to the line at the back of the engine and wait for further instructions. My boss of the day will tell me to pull the line or just get a tool and go into the fire. Since I was the youngest guy on, then I'd always be on the pipe if we stretched our line or another Engines line. This did not bother me; I made up in my mind not to let anything including my boss did get me upset. I was ready for anything, I've accepted the possibility of Death.

We took the rig to the shop to get all my firefighting equipment. The shop was on Russell Street in the Eastern Market. I got a helmet, boots, a fire fighting coat, gloves, air mask, and a flashlight. I put my name on them with a marker and put E-49 ABRAMS on the back of my coat. Now I was ready to fight fires, even though I was a little scared inside. Lt Krolik told me where I was to sit on the fire engine, how I was to respond, and what tools to bring in the fire. I was an engine man so I would be first on the line, if we arrived first. All that day after coming back from the shop I cleaned that engine house from top to bottom. The jobs I did looked like no one else had ever done, like the exhaust fan in the kitchen. There was so much grease on that fan, it looked as if it has never been cleaned since the station was built. I cleaned the walls, the windows, polished the brass pole, and any other brass that needed polishing like the door knobs. Then the alarm went off, Thank God we had a fire.

A box alarm went off at Grand River and Robson , we were the third engine on the run. I jumped on the engine behind Lt Krolick, put on my air tank, looked through the window from the back. We flew down Grand River, the siren was screaming as we blew the horn, riding down the middle lane of the street, cars were pulled over, as we went bye. I was a little bit nervous as I checked my air pressure on my tank. I could see the smoke as we pulled up to the house on fire. It was a two family dwelling a few houses down from a party store. There was a swarm of fire fighters and their rigs in the front with hoses stretched all over the front lawn. When we got to the house the first engine had already arrived stretched lines attacking the fire. The fire was on the second floor, so I ran up the stairs, with my axe in my hand. I was behind a bunch of fire fighters on the stairs, someone yelled that we got some TFF's here so they let us up pass them. The hallway was filled with smoke but there was some visibly. In my haste to get to the fire, as soon as I got to the top of the stairs, I fell in a hole in the floor. There I was hanging to the floor, when I looked up there was TFF Berry, he reached down and pulled me up with one hand. There was a fireman at the top of the stairs that after the next would come up he would say watch-out for the hole in the floor. When I came up the last person didn't tell me so when I went pass the floor I fell right in. I dropped my axe and grabbed the floor hanging on the side. Berry came up right after I did; when he saw me dangling he reached down and pulled me up with one hand. It was a good thing Berry was working at Engine 42 and they arrived right after us. After getting up out of that floor I just walked around and looked, the fire was out so they called us out, Engine 49 is leaving. Since TFF Berry was working at Engine 42 we would be working on a lot of fires together.

On our way home I was thinking about that fire, and how fast my heart was racing, I got to be more careful. Wondering is this me, can I do this work, what's going to happen next. We got back to the fire station, and I put my fire fighting gear up, got it ready for the next fire. I washed up, and went back to work on my project the kitchen exhaust fan. I never cleaned so much grease before, kind of reminded me of cleaning for my father. My father use to say "if you don't clean it right the first time, you got to do the whole job over". The cook came back from shopping, so I let him have the kitchen, a lot cleaner now.

Lt Krolik was a very good cook he would make many meals, home made pies, and other Polish meals, like stuffed cabbage, and stuffed peppers. He would send the cook out to shop for him, and he would do all the cooking. The cook for the day was Leroy, a fire fighter for about five years, he was the first to help me get along with Lt. Krolik. He told me to take my time and when I'm finish just stay out of his way. The way he was getting ordered around I didn't understand, but as time went on I figured it out. Lt Krolik was Archie Bunker, and Leroy was the Meathead. They would have me leave the kitchen

, and do work in other areas of the station. Leroy taught me how to always look like I was working, that way Lt Krolik wouldn't have to find me another job. When I was working at Ford's Transmission Plant, the workers told me how to work. I had a Foreman that would take me from job to job, and he told me that he was going to teach me every job there so I could be a Foreman. The other workers told me to slow down, because I was doing the work of three men. I would stack up a job for three hours, then he would take me to do another, and I would do the same. When some of the workers didn't show up it was the Foreman's job to get that work done. He would come and get me, I learned almost all the jobs there, and I always worked overtime if he asked me. It wasn't that the work was to hard, it was too repetitive for me. I'm not a robot, and it was too boring that's why I quit and went to California.

When lunch was ready they called me in the kitchen to eat. We only had four men today, the boss, a Senior fire fighter cook, the FEO, and the TFF. We had polish sausage with potatoes and onions, and a salad , bread and punch. After lunch I washed the dishes, swept the floor, and mopped it. We ate at 1300 hours, then the fire fighters would sleep till about 1600 hours. When you're running at a fast station you got to get all the rest you can, because you don't know how many fires you would have at night. While everyone was sleeping, when I went on watch Lt Kroilk would have me study the maps. I would study the area that we were in so if someone had a problem finding a street I could help. Always looking for the best and quickest route to the fire.

The crew was upstairs asleep and I had the station to myself. Now I made it, my boss was sleep so I could relax. I walked around the station just looking at everything. It was nice and quiet. I sat at the running board, with all the box numbers that we serviced, and the street locations. The radio was on and it called out all the fires in the city their status, the type of fire who responded, and who's on the way back home. There was a large map on the wall, that had all the street names, and how they ran. Then all of a sudden the alert bell rang, all the lights turned on and the phone rang. I answered it, "TFF Abrams Engine 49 yes" . I was very nervous as I grabbed a pen to write. This is Central Office you've got a run, a fire was reported at 12336 Pinehurst, I repeated the address back to her as I wrote it down. " 12336 Pinehurst, reported kitchen fire" the crew came running downstairs, "we got a kitchen fire on Pinehurst" I gave the piece of paper to the boss, and ran to get my gear. I put on my boots first, then coat and jump on the Engine. Pinehurst was right around the corner; I threw my mask on, and put on my gloves. The front door opened up and we took off, with the siren blasting and the horn blowing. This was it and we were first, we got there so quickly, Leroy told me to go to the back of the engine and wait, while he checked it out. He ran to the door and asked who called the Fire Department, the door was open and the house was smoke filled. Leroy came running out the house with a burning pan and threw it on the front grass. He told me to leave the line and come on in. We opened the windows and aired the smoke out the house, then we checked to see how far the fire got. The fire didn't get very far, it just turned everything black in the kitchen, it didn't get through the walls. When all the smoke was out and we made sure the fire was out, we went back to the station. As I walked outside there was a crowd that formed to see what was going on. I felt good that I actually did something to help someone in need. I finally made it, now doing what I love, I felt fulfilled in life. There were a couple of cute girls in the crowd; I began to like this area. When we got back to the station, everybody went back up stairs to finish their nap. I put up my fire equipment ready for the next fire, I was still on watch, so I washed up and sat back at the running desk.

I just studied the map, looking at the street names. On the way back from runs I would look at the street names and how they ran. Although I grew up in Detroit I didn't know this area well. I've only been over to this area a few times, just to visit. I would write the street name down and how they ran. Every afternoon Lt. Krolick would give me a test on streets, where they were, and how to get to them the fastest. One afternoon we took the rig to Engine 42's house that's where TFF Berry was assigned, his boss was Lt. Sarafinski a buddy of Lt. Krolick. I guess Lt Sarafinski must have been bragging on how good his

TFF was. They took us to the running board and began to test us on the streets. Every street they asked me I knew, where it was and how to get to it. My boss was very happy that day, because he had something he could ride Lt Sarafinski with. That's when he started calling me "the Kid". He saw how I caught on very quickly, and was always eager to please him. I was always very respectful to my boss, just as if he were my father.

Firemen have a certain way about themselves, always in competition, and this made them better. Racing to get to the fire first, and claiming the fire. If they could put it out alone with their engine men they would have bragging rights. You could profess the great adventure, as if slaying a fiery dragon and many did. Each Engine company would have an area they were responsible for, other Engines would try to steal their fires. The Engine that arrives first and hooks up to the Hydrant and gets water can claim that fire. If they can't get water another engine can try at another hydrant, and they can take that fire.

Lt Krolick was a by the book type boss. He wouldn't go of out his way to take a fire, in fact, we would get lost on the way to a fire. Maybe that's why he wanted me to study the map, at first they never asked me which way to a fire. It was late at night we got a run, I was up as soon as the lights came on. I ran to the pole and slid down to the apparatus room. Put on my boots, coat and helmet jumped on the rig, as it started smoke filled the room, Leroy opened the doors, and we pulled out. The siren roared as we flew around the corner, I checked my air mask and turned it on. We rode for blocks and blocks, we turned left then right, as we rode I notice we were going around in a circle. I looked up front and Lt Krolick and the FEO Greluski looked as if they were lost. I liked FEO Greluski he looked like Captain Kangaroo a big nice guy. He was a heavy set older man a least fifty or more with blonde hair and a thick mustache. I think he and the Lieutenant were friends they were both Polish. He was always agreeable and kind. He was a swing Engineer and this area he didn't know well.

They were looking at maps with a light on, trying to find which way to go. Finally we were called in by the radio to go back home. Maybe I was sent here for a reason; this gave me the fever to work harder to help them.

Then I finally had my first good fire. It was about 2200 hours, the alert went off all the lights came on. I was tired by now. I can see how this would get on your nerves, up down up down, here we go again. By this time I don't care who called it in, or where it's at. I just rode until I smelled smoke, wood burning, that means a house fire. When we pulled up it was going through-out a blazing flame coming out the top windows. We were first I ran to the back for instruction, Lt Krolik said "grab the inch and a half". I grabbed the bundle of line and took it to the front door. The house looked vacant. FF Leroy told me to kick the front door because I was a bigger man than him, 6'2" 195 pounds. I put my big number 12 foot on the door with a healthy kick with all my weight. The door flew wide open, it was dark and smoky, Leroy told me to find the fire first before you open the pipe. If you open the pipe before you get to the fire, the whole house will fill up with white smoke, and you won't be able to find it. I put on my mask and we crawled from the first floor to the second, just feeling our way around. We could barely see anything, until *I saw a orange glow in the corner.* It was just like the smokehouse, and with a air mask on it's hard to see anything. Leroy was right behind me as we got closer to the fire. When we got right on the fire everything cleared up and you could see the whole room, where the fire was burning. That's when I opened the hose, and shot the water at the fire. Then I swirled the hose in a circle to hit the four corners of the ceiling then the room. That cooled the room off cause it was hot, real hot. Then I shot the water right at the heart of the fire, it took a while before it when out. I kept hitting the ceiling and walls to so that room wouldn't catch back on fire. After I got that room out I went to another room and did the same thing. The Ladder truck was on the roof I could hear them as they chopped a hole in the roof. Now we could see light from the roof and the smoke could go out through it. After I went to every room blasting water everywhere the fire was out, Leroy told me to go to the window and fog out the smoke. That's when you spray a wide oval stream of water out the window that clears the smoke out. When the smoke clears you can see everything. That's when my job was over. I put the fire out, I did it and, it felt good. There was a very good feeling in my heart, I've made it and I've got the best feeling I've ever had like a natural high. While we were picking up, putting away our equipment, and rolling up the hoses, I felt high that followed me back to the firehouse; I was stepping on clouds, and was all hyped up. My heart was still racing as adrenaline flowed through my body. I never felt like this before like I could do anything. When we went back to the Engine house we talked about the fire, I just listened to everyone else I didn't say a word, but I was happy.

My next working day I worked with another crew. It was Lt Maher in charge, like "Sheriff Andy Griffin," a very nice white man, thin built and soft spoken. My FEO was McPhail a cool southern type, that was like Burt Reynolds, he cared about his rig, and he knew the territory. He was always working on the rig getting it ready for the next fire, painting it, polishing it, checking the tires. My senior Fire Fighter was Felton and he was something else, black thin not so tall, he was like Clevon Little mixed with Richard Pryor. He was always giving me tips on how to fight fires. Always watching out for my safety he was just like my big brother. I guess I've found a new family and we got along excellently, now with this crew we fought many fires. I liked this crew better than the other shift, there was no stress or animosity, we really worked well together. To do a good job you needed a good crew, one that you could count on, and they were it. I feel the reason why TFF's were taken through so much was because they wanted to get rid of quitters, they wanted you to work until you die. On the way back from the fires and when we were riding the rig on the streets Felton would ride on the ladders on top of the engine waving at everyone as we passed and giving out the Black power sign. When we passed any other city workers and black businesses, it was like being part of the Black Panthers like by brother Rod. This is when Felton became my brother and I soon found out he was more like my brother than I would ever know. We had the only Engine truck with these Freeway Ladders that sat right on top of the Rig. We were so close to all the Freeways we had to have these special Ladders, so we could climb down to put out car fires, and evacuate accidents. We fought many fires together back to back all through the night. Felton made sure nothing happen to me he would always say be careful.

The next working day Lt Kroilk was bragging on how I would do anything he said with the other firemen. This is when he told me to take down my pants. I started to take them off when he and Leroy started laughing. He was just playing but he gave me so many orders I would obey without thinking. All I was thinking was why he wanted me to take my pants off. While I was trying to figure out what was going on I found out later that firemen love playing games. They all laughed as I was unbuckling my pants, and looking like a fool. Another day Lt Kroilk wanted to have some fun firemen style. He asked me how many push-ups I could do. "Can you climb up the pole." When I jumped up on the pole a started climbing I saw through the pole covers someone moving. I was almost at the top when Leroy threw a bucket of water down. I jumped off the pole pushing away from the water. The water hit Lt Kroilk right in the face, as he turned bright red. He was so mad as the water dripped from his face. He had to take off his glasses and he was steaming " you got me fool, you were suppose to hit the kid". We all laughed together firemen weren't so bad. I enjoyed fighting fires so much it didn't matter because I couldn't wait till the next fire. Lt Krolik wanted to show me our fire area and how far it went and he liked going to Dearborn so we took a ride. Lt Krolik liked riding the area and visiting the shops talking to the people. We rode the area from Wyoming to Tireman then we went rode to the Dearborn city limit. When we got there to Warren and Wyoming and we went to this Flooring store and when they came out the Engine wouldn't start, and we were in Dearborn out of our area. Now Lt Krolik had to call the shop and tell them where we were. They had to send a tow truck after us. This was the first time that let me see that I was being watched over. Every time that I was misused or abused something would happen to the people that did it to me. This is when I started praying for my crew I worked with no matter what they did. Lord Please don't hurt them. This also made me think maybe there is a God, and he has angels watching over to protect me. We rode with the tow truck to the shop, which was at the Eastern Market. We sat around the shop while they tried to fix our Engine. When they couldn't fix it they gave us an X-rig, this was a old engine that they had sitting around and used when ever they needed. This was also the reason why the Department had problems because they needed more newer Engines, and Trucks. The money wasn't put in the budget so we had to use what was there. They gave us an old covered wagon, this was one seen on old Keystone Cops movies. We could stand on the back running board while riding to fires. Now we had to transfer all the hoses to the X-rig. Now that is work the amount of line carried on a engine took us two hours to change. Now this rig was fun riding on the running board back to the Engine house. When we entered service area we were put in service. When we went back in service we caught a fire, right away. It was a grass fire in a field, on the other side of the tracks off Michigan avenue. Lt Krolik had a lot of good ideas about fighting fires, like the civil reserve canister that we carried on the rig for grass fires. Since this rig doesn't have a high pressure line we carry water. Lt Krolik had me go downstairs and get an old civil defense canister with a hand pump. I filled it up with water and Krolik showed me how to pump the water out. When we had small fires so we wouldn't have to stretch the line we could use the hand pump. After I put that fire out we went back to the Engine House, it was about lunch time now. We got a new man transferred to the station Senior FF Kalunsy he was a younger white, cool guy. We got along real well, he was real nice always telling jokes, a good fire fighter. Leroy would get details out now because Kalunsy had more seniority then he did, I will miss him, because he taught me how to get along with Krolik. Kalunsy would always go out his way getting real expensive food. He would go to a special butcher in southwest Detroit to shop. He had to either spent some of his own money or got a good deal because he was a fire fighter. SFF Kalunsy was the cook today and he made Porterhouse steaks about two inches thick. I wasn't use to eating beef. All the beef I ever had was roast beef, and it was always tough and chewy. We would spit it out in the garbage as soon as my mother would leave the room. We used to chew it so long it wouldn't go down so we had to spit it in a napkin and throw it away. They asked me if I liked steak and I told them no. We had to give the cook four dollars a day, and he would go out to shop at nine o'clock, and get back at eleven o'clock. Since I paid for the food I ate it, to my surprise it was excellent. We had steak, with sauté onions and mushrooms, mash potatoes, green beans, served with French bread, and a salad. The cooks job was very important we need healthy food to keep us in condition to fight fires that could last all night. Engine 49 was a busy house we are always was running from fires to fire. We would get one at about 9 or 10 o'clock , another 11, and 12 o'clock , another one or two after lunch, a couple more in the evening, and at lease three more through the night. After we ate everyone went upstairs to get some rest, because we would never know how many fires we would have that night. They slept for about an hour before we caught another run. I was studying the maps when the alarm came from the telegram system, a bell rang, while it punched out a box alarm. 443 came across that was Grand River at Ilene, we were first. The phone rang I answered it "Fire Fighter Abrams", "you have a box alarm at you have a house fire at 12226 Ilene, it's reported that there are people in the house". I repeated the address back while I wrote it down on a note pad. By this time everybody was down stairs getting dressed putting on our equipment. I gave the paper to the Lt. and he jumped in the rig started the engine opened the doors, and we took off. We were now riding the covered wagon riding the back running board, so I got dressed while I held on. I slipped on my air tank as we got closer, I held a steel bar on the back as we rode to the fire. We had to be careful always have a hand on that steel bar. One slip and you would be on the ground behind the rig, and they won't see you either.

We arrived first I could see the fire in the front of the house as it burned the front porch. Lt Krolick ordered me to stretch the first bed and told Kalunsy to check the house and get everybody out. I grabbed the inch and a half and dragged it to the front porch. I dropped it there took it a loose, spread it out and got it ready for water. The rig went right to the hydrant and hooked up, I got water fast. I first put out the fire on the porch , then I when in the front door and fought the fire on the first floor. The fire didn't spread far it was out quick. When we got finished the streets were full with people crowding all around. There was a mother and her children that were inside they were fine. She told Kalunsy that she just put out her son and he must have set the chair on fire on the porch because he was mad. Fires were started from many different reasons some accidents others intentional.

There was something special about this Grand River, and Meyers area, that made me want to claim them. Like I was assigned to protect them, and not just on my work day. They told us in the academy that we were always on call even if we were off. I got to know some of the neighbors. Freddy knew almost everyone. He was a very happy high strung young man about seventeen years old. Freddy was a fire buff. He would be so fascinated with the work he would hang out all day at the fire station. When he was a little boy he would always be up at the station talking with the firemen, washing their cars, helping with work and running to the store. He was a very different person, he lived for firefighting, he was too afraid to become one, but he loved the Fire department. He knew a lot about the department, the rigs, and equipment, just from being there and helping. He knew a lot of the streets and routes to fires, who would be going on a run, who would show up first. A lot of firemen thought he was slow, but I never did. I learned a lot from him as well as the other firemen. My shift was split, one day with Lt Krolick and FF Jenkins, now Kalunsy, the next day I would work with Lt Maher and FF Felton. There wasn't a day when we didn't have a fire, and many days we would work all day and through the night fighting fires.

My first serious accident happened on my second shift, with Lt Maher and FF Felton. We got the call right before lunch, it was a Box that we were first arriving company. FEO McPhail was driving and he was fast, the call was on Griggs and Schoolcraft. We busted out of the fire station in three minutes after we got the call. He took Pinehurst to Fullerton then made a quick left on Wyoming, across the service drive on I-96 to Griggs. When we arrived I jumped off with my tank on my back, and ran to the back of the rig by the hose bed and bundle. Felton said hold on I'm going to check it out. He ran in to see if their was anyone in the house that needed rescuing first. Lt Maher gave me the order to stretch the line, so I unhooked the bundle. I threw the bundle on my shoulder took it to the door way and opened it. On our first line we had a 20 pound brass Rockwood pipe as my nozzle. Now this was a very good pipe, it would have a good strong straight stream, and you could pop the top off and get a fog spray too. The line started filling with water and I spread the line out so I could get water. By that time Felton came back and said no one inside you can open the pipe. I did and stepped in the door and opened the pipe hitting first the ceiling going from corner to corner in a circular motion. Then coming down to wet the whole room , after putting out one room I went to the next, the kitchen, and did the same thing. We fought our way to the back with Felton right behind me. Then there was a stair way up to the second floor at the back of the house, we started up the stairs with the pipe at full blast. When Engine 30 pulled up to the front of the fire the flames were shooting out the second floor window, facing the street. They thought they were helping us by shooting their water gun in the window, dumping their tank into the house. This gun was like a bazooka and was very powerful; it was connected to the top of the engine, and was very useful on many occasions, but was never to be used with people inside. This was Engine 30 and they had a new rig with new equipment and so they were trying it out. On the inside as we got to the top of the stairs we enter the mouth of the fire, we heard a loud boom. All of a sudden everything came our way. A back draft of Fire, smoke, and steam hit us and knocked us out. I was swept off my feet and the Rockwood pipe smacked me across face as I fell down the stairs. We got to our feet and stumbled out the house, It was like a auto pilot that guided me out as we bumped into walls trying to find my way out. A fire fighter saw me in the front room coming from the back, he said "you're bleeding, your face." I felt the warm blood as it dripped down my face. Not knowing where I was, or the condition I was in dazed and confused, some other firemen came to our rescue, they helped me to the door. I was out on my feet still walking. Lt Maher called an EMS to take me to the hospital. They were there within minutes and they drove me off, while I looked thru the window. My mind wandered as I thought about holding the record for the most stitches in the hood. I went to the hospital more times than anyone on our street.

There is something about when a firemen goes to the hospital, first we smell up the place. After coming out of a fire of course we smell just like fire. I filled the ER with the odor of smoke, when all the doctors, and nurses passed me would say where's the fire. The EMS put gauges on the wound and stopped the bleeding in the truck, on the way there. The Doctor went to work right away, he put eight stitches on the inside and thirteen on the outside. Everyone was nice to me at Northwestern hospital the nurses were flirting, and I enjoyed my reception. I called my mother to come get me, and they were there in no time. I felt real good but it was something I didn't like staying in the hospital no longer than I had to. When I got home I called my girl friend and she came over, and treated me to a Hero's delight. The best thing about getting hurt in a fire is all the attention. Ramona knew how to treat a man. If I had any brains I would have married her. She was so sweet and fine as can be, when you went out with her you knew you were special. Being a young man I had no idea how to work a real relationship no one ever explained this to me. I asked my father how would I know if I was in Love. The true answer is Love is a decision not a feeling.

That pleasure you feel when you see or are with a woman or girl are your senses not love. Many women can make you feel good, but that's not Love it's fondness, favor, or a strong like. When you start to do things that you don't want to just to please them this can become Love. It takes two for Love is a two way street. This knowledge about love may take your whole life to learn, and some have lived and never known real Love. Love is a gift.

All I knew is what I saw at home, what I learned in the streets, and how I felt in my heart. Which didn't amount a thing useful that could help me in my relationship. I had so many doubts about myself. Could I match up to the expectations of my desires? Maybe my dreams were unattainable, there are no perfect men or women. I was a fool because I weighed a woman by a sum of their parts. The real value is in the mind and desires, Ramona loved me and would of done anything I asked. I was too young to understand and she was too hot and intelligent to wait on me. She knew if I didn't act right she would move on because she was a brick House.

I was off for about two months before they were ready to put me back to work. The days that I was off I enjoyed myself, as much as I could. I started a new life philosophy. Do what ever you can to enjoy life at it fullest because tomorrow you never know I might die. After that every off day was spent having the time of my life.

After the experience I had in California I didn't know if there was a God or not. I blamed God, and especially

Jesus for what I went through at that Holiness Church. I struggled to understand if their was a God or not. In my compensations I felt that if there was not a God or Jesus the teachings were good, even if they weren't true. I liked helping people; I would always do things to help those in need, that was just me. In School we were told that Darwin was our God, and that we just formed ourselves out of a one cell organism that crawled out of the water and through evolution changed from a monkey into a man. I never believed that because our bodies were created with intelligent design, there are too many systems working together with a supreme knowledge. How can we say that we created ourselves. I did know what I was doing on the Fire Department was right, and it was for me. All the stories I heard about Jesus I loved, David I loved, and if they are real or not I will still go on to living my life doing good deeds. Saving people and fighting fires was the best thing I could do, when I worked I was the best, and when I was off I had the best time I could. I accepted death, or the reality that I could die in a fire.

I was confused with God when I was a young child. I asked God to speak to me so I would know he was real. I made a promise if he gave me the talent I would spread his word throughout the world. Well my talent never came I played a saxophone, but never got higher than the roady in my brothers band. My brother was one of the best bassist in Detroit, he was always playing music. He started early in school with woodwinds, and went to almost every instrument made. I was changed from clarinet to saxophone then to Baritone because I couldn't keep up, and it was suppose to be easier. My skills never got to where I could be proud of them. I played for my enjoyment in hopes that one day I would be good.

My trial period had passed by, and now I get my badge, I'm a real Fire fighter. At the engine house they started letting me cook. I enjoyed that my mother had already taught me some recipes. Lt Krolik took me to the store and showed me how to shop, he would go to the store with the rig and get a lot of free food. The stores would give firemen the food that was about to go bad, mostly produce. Lt Krolik liked to cook; in fact he would do everything if you let him. He taught me how to make apple pie, we got a case of apples from the market which I had to peel them of course. I learned a lot of recipes from the firemen. I ran into Diana at the market and we flirted with each other. She was so fine I just loved to see her. She was a very good friend of my girl friend Ramona because we had not officially broken up even though we didn't see each other on a regular basis. I don't know what made my life change so much, my girlfriend and I have grown apart. What I was most happy with before I started finding many small things that I didn't like about her. I should have married her but I didn't. Why didn't I marry her? Ignorance simple and plain, if she had of pushed me slowly. I was shy and haven't had enough relationships for me to distinguish what to do correctly. I was waiting for a

10. Ramona was a 9 ½. Long ago I saw a cartoon about a dog and a bone. The dog crossed a bridge while walking he happen to see a refection in the lake. It looked like a dog with a bigger bone than his. His ignorance had him to dive in after the other bone. The dog ends up with no bone at all. The way I broke up with girls was to just stop seeing them, no words, no fighting, if you did something I didn't like I wouldn't call you any more. Since there were so many other girls in Detroit, a big city, I might not run into them till a year later, and because we had no words there was no bad feeling.

Chapter 5

MOVING ON MY OWN

I FOUND OUT THAT A working man is much more attractive to the Detroit women. I can't say if it was the job, maybe it was just the season, or just that I was spending lots of money. It seems like everyone found a way to get in on it. Now my life as a fireman was everything to me, all of what ever I wanted is now satisfied. No more dreams of flying to the moon, or flying a plane. Now my life is on fire and I love it. When at work, or off when I saw a fire I would pull over put on fire boots, coat and helmet and run in to help.

One day while driving around Livernois and Davison, O the writer, and my brother Con were in my van I saw a fire and I took off for it. They asked me where I was going and I said to the fire. When I got there I put on my fire equipment and ran in. This was a fire in a Drug house in the Russell wood District right off Livernois and when they were trying to enter the house gun fire started to shoot off. Everyone jumped behind cars on the street as the shots rang out. The police arrived and it was like a gang war, the fire fighters couldn't get to the fire with the shooting. We waited till the shots stopped before we ran into the house. We fought the fire from the first floor to the second then we found out that it was ammunition in the closet that was going off. After it was knocked down I went back to my van took off my equipment and went where I was going. My brother said "you're crazy, you are off, let them fight that fire." I said "as long as I'm a fire fighter and I past a fire that may need help I will help." On my day off I would work for any firefighter for cash or day-for-day exchange. Many fire fighters called me and had me work while they would do their other job. Like TV Chetham and fire fighter that shoot video on his day off. I would end up going to almost every Fire station in Detroit. I would get $200 per 24 hour day, I guess it's like ten dollars an hour. I didn't care about the money, I just loved the fire department and fighting fires. I was a mercenary fire fighter willing to work many days just to battle the flames.

Fighting fires was like a drug that I was hooked on, and every chance I got I would run in. I was now driving a Ford work van, customized to my specifications, which includes a seven piece pit couch with lamp and table, and my fire equipment in the back. When I was out in California I rode in a customized van of Eric Graham. (

Larry Graham's younger brother) This is what made me want a van, his was so sharp, television, captain's chairs, table, circular windows, crushed velvet Green with orange and a beautiful mural on the outside.

Moving out my parents house into a home of my own while keeping my job is my new test. The only way to be a man is to act like a man. "If you can't follow my rules you can't live in my house" that's what my father told my brother when he kicked him out. My father rented me the house on Griggs for two hundred dollars a month. I felt the best way for me to enjoy this world was by have all the fun I could on my days off. I wanted to be a playboy. My role model of happiness was Dean Martin as Matt Helm. I thought that would make me the happiest, so Griggs Street became the Players Club. Some of my best friends moved in with me, all Players. There was O the writer, Yah-Yah the Muslim, his brother Marcus the con, my brother D the musician and Ross the executive. My brother D and Yah-Yah were the pretty boys and the rest of us were gamers. At that time I implemented the quota , which was three different women per day. I was working on a theory that it took three different women to keep one man, me happy. I was the only one that could keep that quota or even tried. I guess after that time with Kathy that I cried about losing Brenda she took me to her house and told me there were more fish in the ocean. She was thirty—five and I was only eighteen at the time, and she was the finest I'd ever seen. I tried to settle with her but she knew that it wouldn't work and she told me to enjoy her while it last. That might have been only one night but it's lived in my heart for years. How I wish I could of married her. I was too young to know a thing about Love or women.

The real reason I stopped looking for a real relationship, was because every time I opened up my heart it was stomped on. The more I didn't care for a lady the more she loved me, when ever I fell for her, I was getting dumped next. I made it a point not to fall for anyone no matter how fine and beautiful. Then came Robin, my brother had met a nice young lady named Page. A very nice and smart young lady with braces. She had a friend named Robin, I didn't know she liked me until one day she right out of the blue she kissed me. I was stunned she was too fine for me light brown long hair light brown, she was like a dream come true. The problem was that she was so fine that all my friend were trying to talk to her. My buddy Yah tried to pull her right in front of my face. She picked me, so of course I was interested, but her beauty scared me. The chase was on we had some good times but like every fine young lady they might start the race but not make the finished. After men show interest they fade to black and let you chase them around the world. I was just stunned that she chose me, there is no way that she could ever take that first kiss away from me. That was the day when this drop dead gorgeous young lady make a pass at me. It was all so innocent and deliberate, she had to been talking about me. What is it that make beautiful women just have to kiss me. They love to fall in my arms, if I could only keep one.

I have learned to be happy with what life brings you. To find love you must lose love. By not looking for love it will find you.

Who can figure women or love out, so I stopped trying and started having fun. For some strange reason I was in season and not just white women this time. It had to be the job because I met so many at work. I was found to be desirable to most women I meet.

I guess because I was meeting some of the most beautiful women in Detroit and they were interested in me. Was it my job, my car, my love van, or that I always had money, and was always spending it on my crew, and the women, I never knew such enjoyment. Those days I always had a lot of friends, Butch Freddie Dog and the Monica crew, O the writer from the eastside, Yah—Yah and his brother Marcus the Muslim brothers, Jesse my brother D, DJ, Darren Martin and his boys, Daryl and Clyde, Garcia and his girls Toya, Loren, and Tijuona just to name a few. I moved back to the house I grew up in on Griggs. First I had to kick out our last tenants, who weren't paying the rent. I called my buddies Butch and Freddy-dog, and a couple of other Big Fellows like DJ, and Maccott Construction Crew. When they all showed up at our house, and we had no trouble moving them out. I heard later that our old tenants were killed and put in a vehicle with their hands tied behind their back and heads cut off. (But that's a different story)

It felt good to move back into the house I grew up in, my heart had never left this street. We moved to a better neighborhood, because my mother saw that things were getting rougher and more crime was happening there and she made my father move. When we moved into the University District it was going through a change one or two Black families move on a street. Then most of the white families started to move out. The Real Estate companies were playing dirty pool, calling and the owners and telling them that the property was going to go down because blacks are moving in. We got our house at a steal my mother made a low ball offer of twenty nine thousand and they accepted it. Mostly Teachers lived in the U of D area and that was the reason it was so well kept. When we moved in we were the third Black family now on the street, by the end of the year there was only five white families left. I had friends from my old street that I missed, although I had a lot of new friends too.

Now I didn't have to sneak girls into the basement of my parents house. I remember one day after picking up Karen from Cass High school, I ran into some old friends, Neskie, Audrey, Nancy, and Brenda my old girl friend. Brenda saw that I was trying to talk to Karen so she got jealous after dumping me. I was still cool with her, even though Karen was finer she was still looking good. She was wearing a vest and blue jean, back then everybody wore blue jeans. We went to Northland Mall and just hung out walking around, all the time Brenda was riding me. She liked to call me ugly, and disagreed with everything I was saying, she was trying to make me look bad in front of Karen. I was just walking and talking with Karen but Brenda would jump in between us with her rude remarks. I just played her game and laughed at everything she did, while she was picking in my hair, and doing anything to bother me. When we left the Mall I dropped Neskie and her girlfriend at her house. Brenda lived in between Neskie house and mine. Karen lived on my street so I was going to drop her off last. Brenda asked Karen don't you got to go home first, so Karen agreed with her, and I said OK. I took Karen home and Brenda jumped up front and said I got to use the bathroom.

I took her to my house and showed her the bathroom, when she got finished I stood at the doorway and waited. When she came out I told her you need to button up your cloths, so she unbutton her vest two more buttons. She came out with a couple of buttons lose and I could see her breast. She had the type that would fit in a champagne glass, European and they were very beautiful. All she had on was a vest and no bra, she was light skinned like pink champagne. I said don't you think you should button that up. I was trying to be faithful to Karen, but we weren't even together yet. She proceeded to unbutton her vest, as I reached in and started to kiss her. She asked me if I had a more comfortable place we could go, I took her straight down stairs. I started by sipping her pink champagne, and she unzipped my pants, as we fell right onto the couch in her favorite position. Brenda's nick name was BJ, and I know why she was the best. I will always love Brenda my first love, she was such a nymph. I have Brenda to thank about my sexual skills, she taught me everything I knew as we practiced all the positions. Even though she was younger than I, she had more experience, because all I did was lie about having sex. I really knew nothing until I met her. Like love went with me as soon as I was happy and ready to settle down it was over. She got rid of me because she was too fast and I was too slow. We were making love for about thirty minutes and my sister called me from upstairs.

I put on my cloths and went upstairs my sisters told me that Angie is at the side door and Karen's at the front door and Tonya's on the phone. I said you know I'm not here, and went back down stairs to finish what I started. My Van was parked right out front so they knew I was there, but I didn't care. I was back with Brenda my first Love, and I was going to enjoy her as much as I could. I was mixed up or my heart was I would have been happy with Brenda, but she was just using me. She use to tell me I was ugly I just had a perfect body, and she Loved my body. Brenda wasn't the finest, but to me she was everything, the type I was crazy about, smart, wore glasses. I really never thought I could get a girl like Karen. I tried to marry them both but they weren't thinking about that, they just wanted to have fun. I guess after having a girl as fine as Karen, smart, and a real gamer, everyone would turn their heads when she would come in the room. I dreamed of marrying someone like Brenda or Karen. It really hurt me that I couldn't marry someone I wanted, Ramona wanted to marry me but I wasn't ready to marry her.

Why was I ready to marry someone that was light skinned with light brown hair, but not ready to marry the brown skin young lady. It must have been as my friend O told me, I was going for girls that reminded me of my mother. Maybe it was that I went for beautiful girls that I couldn't get and that made the chase better. There was no chase with Ramona. It was like we both knew that we were for each other and their was no questions about it. She was the type that just knew the right thing to do. After having Brenda and meeting Karen it would be hard to settle for Ramona, it probably would have been safer, but I don't know if it would of lasted. Brenda was not the finest she was real plain wore glasses and there was no chase with her either. I would of married her at the drop of a hat. The fact was that I had no idea what I wanted.

Then one day I was at Hudson's in Northland Mall with Ramona and I almost got caught talking to Karen upstairs working, while Diane was in perfumes, Elecia was on the first floor, and Angie in the basement she worked there also. Ramona and I were just friends at this time we stayed in touch even when we were apart. I took her over my girlfriend's Elecia's house to meet her. Then we went to the mall. I was friends with many ladies in the store, in fact this was my favorite store. Two girls I knew approached from different directions while I was talking to Ramona. I took off right out the door before I got caught in the middle of them. O just stood with Ramona and laughed as I ran out. In fact I used to pick up so many women at Hudson's I had at lease four that I went out with all on different floors and in different sections. That's when I knew it was really over, between Ramona and me. I don't know why but it went on just a little longer. We were both seeing other people but it was hard really breaking up. We created a bond though we were looking for another mate, we still cared for each other. She was at the time living with another man. This is what told me that I should of married her. We were both in different relationships, but she still found time to check on me. We talked about our relationships and what we were doing. Elecia later found out that I like Karen and she told me if I wanted her go ahead and try. She knew her from school and knew she had a boyfriend. Elecia was just as fine as Karen in fact she was finer. She had hazel eyes that would change colors. She was a Jamaican girl who loved to dance. She was my dream girl, my soul mate. What was real special we had history. I knew her when she was a child. I saw how she was raised. Her mother was like my mother, they knew each other. Our families were friends my brothers were cool with her brothers.

Now she was the perfect girl I should have married. She was fun intelligent and very demanding, she reminded me of my sister. When I was very young Elecia's brother was the paperboy. He used to give us a ride on his bike. Her mother looked just like mine. She had two brothers that were friends with my two brothers. I looked up to her brothers they were very intelligent. When we used to walk to school everyday Elecia would be playing outside on her tricycle. She looked like little orphan Annie, in the comic paper. She has always been like a little sister to me, even after we stopped going together we still stayed close. If she needed me to help her I would be there in a flash, because she was my girl! Someone that fine had to have some bad qualities. Like in the morning she was as mean as a mountain lion. She was just a little too strong willed for me, but her advice was always good. Controlling and a little smarter than I, the problem was she was always correct. She lived right around the corner from Griggs street. Much finer than the twins both put together. They lived right behind her. She was going to Wayne State for fashion design, she made her own clothes. I said that I would stop seeking Karen. I knew she had a boyfriend. I did, but she was still in my mind even if I didn't see her. She was going off to school this fall anyway. A smart way to plan my life was to picture a future with whom I wanted to settle down with. Take what they wanted to do in life and see if it would work with my career. Love is a two street. It takes two to tango. This is when I learned to be happy with whoever is digging me at the time. It makes no sense to chase after something I can not obtain. Yes I will try but if I see no response, then let it go. I can be happy with a worthy attempt, at lease I tried.

I used the Darwin Theory of selective dating the strongest will survive. This way my children will be better prepared to deal with the world because, they would be stronger, smarter, and adaptable. My genes will match with other superior gene traits. I learned this in the Detroit public school system. The same school system taught us that God is just a religious belief, like a fairy tale, or a myth. The primitive man believed in Gods like the Norsemen, Greeks, and Romans, to do the things they were unable to accomplish.

In hunting for the best quality it is better to become organized. We ran our Player's house like a corporation. Each morning on Griggs Street we would get the line up, on who's coming over, and what time. It was like business meeting at the boardroom " Who you got coming Yah, what time" . Yah and I were the best pullers, but sometimes my brother D and O did well also. The groups of girls were like a revolving door everyday someone different. Girls would come out in groups for safety, but we had a system, by pairing up, we could get them alone. If you didn't like them they would stay in the living room. If they didn't want to do anything they would stay in the living room until their friend were finished. When they would go to the bedroom that was their way of showing their approval. Sometimes we would get new guests before we were finished with the other ones. One time I had to sneak a girl out though the window so the new girls in the living room wouldn't see her. Who just happened to be my sisters best girlfriend Margie. A very nice looking sweet girl, light skinned with long dark hair. She had these big fat lips that were gorgeous. She had been trying to get her hands on me, for a while so I thought I would let her. She wore braces and was very cute, and fast, I always had to slow her down. One time she cornered me in a closet and gave me a hickey. I was so embarrassed; I had to cover it up for a week. Well this time I didn't stop her. I let her do what she wanted to do, and we had fun, but just like all the other fast girls they weren't being tied down. I never tried to, I guess after seeing that's how it goes I just went with it. She was into doing strange things, and I didn't mind the experiment, I'm new at this game so I learned. We had to keep this a secret because we didn't want my sister to know, I guess that's why she went with the set-up. After walking her to her car I kissed her goodbye and walked into the house like I just got there. Because my brothers girl Paige was there with her girlfriend Robin, and she was super fine. I was just nice to super fine girls I really didn't try to talk to them too fast. I just played it nice and slow. All the while my past was there in the back of my head warning me from falling to hard for any one girl. I knew the finer they were the harder I WOULD FALL. Now if a young lady shows interest that's a different story. Yes I was sucked into another beauty that just wants me to chase her without the possibility of catching her. Maybe because I was too slow to attack her and in my stall she grew disinterested. Maybe she was interested just to get Margie jealous. I found out later they knew each other. For some reason Margie thought that Robin and I had got together. I think they went to school together. That was my dream to marry her but I never found out what they were up to, the games girls play. Did they want me or were they just enjoying themselves. It's funny how she one day had a baby by a male dancer, and I could have been the first black man to start male dancing in Detroit. It was at the time Prince was out and started the sexual revolution with Madonna. I was at a fashion show-masquerade party. I was dressed as Prince with an overcoat flaming red Speedo swimming trunks and legwarmers. At the time I was known for my body I would wear shorts to many parties and women would always be pinching my rear end or legs. I know how that can be very annoying. I was trying to win the prize for best costume. During the fashion show they just happen to put a song on by Prince. That's when I jumped on the top of a table opened my trench coat. A crowd of beautiful women, yes some were full figured converged at my table screaming. They pulled money out and started stuffing it all over while I was dancing on the table. Now this could have been the start of male dancing in Detroit. When they saw all the women and how quickly they gave there money up to a good looking man. They knew this would be a good profitable business. I was asked to come on the local dance show and appear at the Latin Quarter as a regular. I turned them down it I thought at the time that it was beneath me.

I give the most respect to the finest women even if they didn't want me to. I learned when I cared too much for a woman and respected them, I lost them just as quick. I really cared for most women and it was hard to get me to treat them like lower class street women. Everyone else went crazy for them but I kept my head. I did think about making a mistake and getting them pregnant on purpose, just to keep them. I could never do this dirty trick, if they didn't want to commit to me I would let them go, no matter how much it hurt. I guess I still got morals. I don't know how I kept my morals after losing my God. What I was taught while growing up did mean something to me, even if it wasn't true.

I stop using physical beauty as a prerequisite to start a relationship, and started looking at other qualities. After being hurt by women I tried to talk to regular girls hoping that the relationship would last long. I used to be the one that would go for the finest girl in the room. After many let downs and disapprovals I started talking to women that wanted my attention. I felt more confident with talking to just pretty girls instead of super fine women. I found a new type of women not just the long hair light skinned, light eye beauties that I've been falling for. I started to see the beauty in dark brown, caramel, tan, pink, and freckles, and this was like a new world. Social standing made no different I liked classy women but personalities and how we interact set the stage.

Then we would have road trips in my customized van the first long trip was to Ann Arbor for a party. Ann Arbor was about a thirty to sixth minute trip, on the University of Michigan campus. There was something special about Ann Arbor because it was a learning institution the type of people or students you would run into were free thinkers. All types were there from, hippies, to young scholars, there was no prejudices all people cared about each other. There were musicians, painters, Engineers, Political strategist, young genius, Athletic stars all coming together, some of the greatest new minds converge in one place. This created a magnet that pulled all kinds of Free thinkers, my brother went there to live. Ann Arbor was our magical never never land where we could run away. O the writer had a party that he wanted to take the Warlord sisters. These where two fine girls from the dark arts, they were two witches. Cathy the older sister was into Taro cards and magical spells, the younger sister Kim was just a quite beauty, both deep into the occult. I was interested in the occult also, because I was looking for the meaning of life. I was also studying mental heath, while a researching ESP, higher intelligence, and athletic excellence. O was known for traveling in large entourages with beautiful women that he would assemble on the way there. I started the trip with O the writer, then I picked up my side kick Darren. In school he was the Man everyone knew him as Marrrrrtin, my sidekick and best friend. He would help me with everything, from driving to fighting, if I would drop my wallet or leave the keys somewhere he would follow me and retrieve them. He was the man on the spot, and he always had clever saying. Like turning a sharp corner he would say "Whip it". We picked O up and were on the way to picked up Jeff, he was a con man a real hustler, and trickster. O and Jeff both grew up on the eastside. Jeff was like my younger brother to get money he would sell fake drugs. Darren was a drummer of a band with Clyde playing Guitar and Daryl playing bass and they were good. When Darren saw Jeff he told me that he had sold Clyde some fake Mescaline. Then we picked up the Warlord sisters who always wore black, and both were fine dark brown girls. Kathy wore a medium natural, and Kim had long dark hair that came down pass her shoulders, they lived in Highland Park. We stopped at a beer and wine store on 6 mile and Fairfield Pelzer's Party store and Darren ran into AJ from Mumford they planned to jump Jeff. All they wanted me to do was just pull in front of the University of Detroit's playfield. When I got there AJ pulled the door open and jumped Jeff with three other guys. It all happen so fast that O and I were outside on the side of the van talking about what happen. We laughed then said we got to stop it before it goes too bad. Now AJ and his friends and Darren were all beating Jeff.

The girls were screaming and we came around the van and started pulling off the guys. I grabbed them one by one throwing them off, while O was behind me and kept pulling my arm, while I was pulling these guys off Jeff.

One by one I threw them out my van, five big guys. When I got to the bottom of the pile it was Darren and Jeff, I stopped him. Jeff had rolled into a ball. Then Jeff jumped out of his ball and threw a flying fist right into Darren's jaw. It was just O and I standing at the door when we got them all out and then Jeff still swinging knocked O and I out of the van backwards and we hit the ground. I got the other guys to leave with AJ, and we jumped in the van and took off. All the girls were mad at O, like it was his fault, Jeff just got caught up in some of his own mess. The fault was all mine, but I felt he got what he had coming.

We went on to the party, we picked up Susan, and Antrice, then drove to Ann Arbor. When we got there they wouldn't let O in the party because of what happened in Detroit. We still found another party and had a good time. When the party was over we went by a graveyard on the way home. The night was still young so we thought we would have some fun in the graveyard. We rode around the graveyard and stopped in the middle and drank and smoked for about an hour. When it was time to go I drove around the graveyard and played like we couldn't get out. We stopped again and walked around the graves, and told stories and jokes all night. When the morning came we left I dropped everyone home, Susan was the last girl to get home. I was driving, and Darren was sitting shot gun we all were tired we were drinking all night. I laid my head down for a while and I woke up with someone punching me in the face. I tackled this person that was attacking me, with a shoulder block and he hit the ground with me on top of him in the shrubbery. I then got up and picked him up and threw him in the bushes in front of their apartment. Susan was screaming don't hurt him, he attacked me and she was crying for me to let him go. At the time my van was rolling down, West Grand Boulevard with no driver. Darren woke up and jumped under the driver's wheel and slowed it down and they looked out and saw me fighting with Buford, Susan's husband. Now wasn't nobody trying to talk to her we were all friends. He must of thought that I was my brother, and he heard that my brother was talking to Susan. I jumped back into the van and took off, when I got home we saw a shoe on the floor. We laughed when we got home on Griggs, and O said that I probably knocked him right out of his shoe. We couldn't believe Susan crying out not to hurt him and he was attacking me.

Our next trip was to Chicago to see Heat Wave and Rufus this time with some girlfriends of mine. It was Neskie and her girlfriend Wendy, Darren and O as we left for Chicago. We had no tickets but O was used to getting in to concerts, we would always find a way in. It was a long trip there, five hours, I drove the whole way and when we got there Darren drove around the city. All we needed was a map and we found everyplace and did a little site seeing too. We drove down by the river went the art institute and a bar. We got to the concert hall in time, and then we split up to get in. Darren, O and I went to the back stage door with

O's gift of gab. We went to the will call and he got us some tickets. We got in the concert with plenty of time, it was a excellent facility. Neskie, and Wendy went to where the groupies hung out waiting to see the stars. When Heat Wave appeared through the curtains they were doing acrobatics, the lead singer flipped out to the stage. Their hit single at the time was "Always and forever." They came out on a natural high something like I've never seen before. The stage was a round revolving stage so no matter where you sit it was a good seat. When Rufus came on with Chan ka Kahn as the lead singer it was her daughter's birthday, and she sang a special song to her. It was an excellent night and when it was all over we waited for Neskie and Wendy and they told us they were going to their hotel, so we went there and waited. A bad ice storm hit and we were stuck out in the van all night. The ice was so bad the whole van was covered with ice about three inches thick. Darren was in the back under the covers shaking, O and I were sitting up front. We gave the cognac to Darren to warm him up, because we had to wait till the girls got back before we could leave. The girls hung out with the band all night and came out in the morning. I was mad because I thought they came to be with us, but it turned out they enjoyed the band better. It was the band they wanted we were just second choice. I found out my girl wasn't interested in me at all. Well I can't always get the girls, this time the Heat Wave was more popular than I. This time the concert was one of the best I've seen. I couldn't get mad at Heat Wave for keeping our girls all night.

My next long trip was with Butch to upper Michigan. Lele was enrolled at Western Michigan University in Kalamazoo Michigan. This was Butch's girlfriend so we had to go and visit her. Butch and Lele were my friends that spend the night with me when I got stood up for my Prom by Kiki Dee. We hung out in Windsor all night and they tried not to let me be too depressed, we went to pinball halls playing all night. This was the first time I wore my favorite suit my mother made for me but every time I wore it I got in trouble. The plan was for us to wear blue jeans to the prom when my date was a no show. I called her on the phone to let her know we were on the way. When we got there her father said she went to sleep. She had a real mean father and we thought he didn't want her to go with us. Well I guess I was about used to being kicked in the head. We went anyway don't ask me how but Butch talked me into it going. I tried to have fun but I was too depressed. I was used to being the third wheel.

The ride to Kalamazoo was a three to four hours drive almost as long as the Chicago trip. There was fog on the road on the way up there that was real thick. When we got there we went to Lele's Dorm room, and met her roommates. It was a lot different than Ann Arbor, you could feel the prejudice there. They had a black side and a white side of town. We noticed after going to a black bar that most of the blacks acted like they were from down south. Real slow and stupid almost backwards, I never saw so many ignorant acting black men. We had this same type in Detroit we called them the Jits. While we were at the club Butch was trying to talk to this guys girlfriend. He asked me to distract the guy so he could talk to her. I was talking to this guy and Butch took her out of the dance floor. Before we left the club I needed to distract him again so he could get her number. Butch got the number but he got caught too! We had to hurry up and get out of there while the guys friends were holding him back. It was something about Butch he didn't care if the girl was with someone, it made her more interesting for him.

The trip to Lansing with my protégé Ross was like a trip to the Outer Limits. Ross and I went to an Icebreaker at Michigan State in Lansing, only an hour drive from Detroit. Ross and I were going for the parties. I had been there before because I went there with my mother in the summer for their 4 H Youth programs. When we got there we found the party and enjoyed it. They had Alpha Dogs doing their frat stomp performance, in one of the gyms on the stage, and we walked around meeting young ladies. We danced and partied for three hours, and decided to leave, but when we stepped out it had started raining real hard. We walked these two girls we just met to there dorm. We hung out with them for a while a few kisses goodnight. When we went to find our van, but it was raining so hard. We couldn't walk in it, and we didn't know where we were going. We were walking for a while and wasn't getting anywhere. We got lost and walked around a building about two times. We were lost and it didn't seem like we would ever find it, finally found the van and went home. That was our first rain trip, our second was when we went to Belle Island for a picnic, Ross, Beverly, Angie, and I. On a beautiful summer day found a place out by the water right next to the golf course. We sat down and ate and was having fun, when a dark cloud came over, and everything got dark. We started to get all our stuff together, and it started raining and it came down hard. We were stuck out there and we ran under a tree and stayed there until it slowed down. Angie and I were on one tree, and Ross and Beverly were on another one. We told them the tale of when we got lost in Lansing, in the rain. There was an episode of the Outer Limits that was just like our adventure.

My brother D had been getting into trouble so we sent him out of town, he had a best friend in New Orleans going to school. This just happened to be right before Mardi Gras, on the way down we stopped at Karen's school Tuskegee in Alabama. I found her at the dorm, and she was surprised to see me. We took some pictures, and went to a party together. I ran into another friend that used to party at Studio 54, Park Hotel, and other clubs in Detroit. Karla a beautiful light brown model with long dark brown hair. We also took many picture together, and hung out. Then we went to New Orleans and this was my first time there, we rode down on listening to the B52's, Madonna, and Blondie's music. Many use to say that my brother and I look like twins and would call us that. He was a little lighter than I and had sharper features, light brown curly hair. Yes he was much better looking than I, by what the women say. Women would just throw themselves at him he would only have to pick. He never chased women he was only chased. From him I learned how to notice who was interested in me and enjoy them.

Instead of the constant rejections this was nice, then I learned other more aggressive tactics. New Orleans was excellent, the music, the parties, the Mardi Gras, the parades people drinking in the street. Women pulling up their tops to show their breasts, just for beads CRAZY. They were drinking till they fell out, and while we stood in the streets, and cleaning crew would go right by cleaning up everything. This was a very clean city. I met a few ladies that I cared about, one was real sweet and she lived in Mobile, Alabama. A light brown thin young lady with hazel eyes. She was attending Dillon University this was her lent season. I didn't want to leave she was so sweet. The other girl I met reminded me of the Detroit women but slicker and much wiser. I enjoyed her also but I was very careful. I didn't care too much for wild super hot mamas. Now she was fun and I love dancing, we partied and when it was all over I wanted more. I had to get back to my job I was soon to be on call.

When I got back in Detroit I found out that I had a secret admirer. That was always asking my cousin Diego about me. I really didn't know her but she started speaking to me as she passed. She had sisters that I knew but she was the youngest in the family. My cousin told me about her. Rumor was that she was mistreated by her mother and kept in a closet. I heard many rumors about her but I didn't know who she was. I really felt for her, but just as a friend to see if I could help in any way. She told everyone that she had a crush on me but she was too young for me I think she was fourteen. Her name was Tokey and I knew a lot of her family because they lived down the street from us. Her mother heard how she felt about me and made a big deal to let me know that she was too young and I better not mess with her. Now this is one person I had no intentions of ever messing with. By someone admiring me so much this did something to me. I don't know why I was always contacted by mothers telling me not to mess with their daughters that I didn't know. There were also the twins that lived around the corner, I remember saying that they were fine one day. The next thing I knew their mother came to my door and cursed me out and demanded I better not touch them. I had no plans to mess with these young girls there was so many women of age why would I bother with them. They were fine and twins but they have to be interested in me first for something to happen. I just said that they were fine that's all.

Brenda was the youngest girl I talked to she was 15 when I was 18, and her parents knew my age. There were so many beautiful young ladies in Detroit between 18 and 35 that I would never have time for any underage girls. Now there were younger girls that were around like Tammy, she was a friend of Tokey's. We all lived on Griggs. I became friends with all of her girlfriends. She had a lot of friends and most of them were young and cute. I used to take them to the park, I had a convertible Lemans and we would go to Palmer Park in that or my van, I would take the whole group of girls. Out of the group at lease three Lydia, Regina, Ruth, ended staying friends with me later after they got older and finer. She would always travel with a large group of girls at lease five or six. I was like their older brother at first, I never tried to talk to any of her friends then. I made sure that they were all safe. Tammy was my girl since she was a little girl, I used to carry her on my shoulders. She was always the cutest little girl. Even after she grew up we both knew she was too young and not to try it. She grew to become so fine. I grew up with her, and looked out for her. Her mother and I were cool, she let us make her garage a club house for my gang. I had looked out for Tammy as she got older and she would come to my house just to hang out. At the age of fourteen she was the finest young lady that developed to look like she was twenty. It was tempting after she evolved while getting older. One day we did end up in the bathroom messing around, but it didn't go no further than that. Plus I had a strict moral up bringing. The only reason I talked to so many women was because I was scared of getting hurt. I thought the numbers would save me, they didn't. I guess that was why I liked hanging with them because we were friends and weren't trying to date each other. I was honest with the young ladies I would talk to, and they knew that I wasn't looking for a serious relationship just fun. I was too young for a serious relationship and my desire was to become a Player. I thought a player would never get a broken heart. I found out later that I could become a Player, but Player's hearts get broken too!

When I went back to work a three weeks after the accident and Lt Maher looked at my stitches and said they weren't healed. He sent me back to the Medical Department and told them to give me some more days off. He wasn't going to let me work with my head in that condition. I knew that he cared for me and what a good boss he was. My next work day coming up I would go back to work will now start with Lt Krolik. This was always a hard day cause this Boss always made it one. There was always extra work that he would dream up every dirty job that no one else would do. This made me regret going back to work but after being off for a while

I missed everyone, even Lt Krolik. Yes this was the best place for me, Lt Krolik loved me just like my father. This was his way if showing it, just like my father I would never understand. He could have been like other Bosses that didn't teach their TFF anything. My Bosses made sure that I knew everything they did, they weren't lazy. When I was told that I was going to Engine 49 they said it was fast and I would learn the best there. My Bosses were the best also, to be at this station because we were alone they had to make plenty of hard decisions quick, with knowledge.

My stitches were healed, thirteen right over my eye seven on the inside. Taking that Rockwood brass pipe to my head really knocked me out. I was beginning to feel like Frankenstein the monster. Now it looked like I got a permanent black eye. While sitting around looking at all the other fire fighters that got hurt. I started to see the dead side of the department. This is when I saw fingers missing and injuries that couldn't be fixed. Men that were not able to come back to work. How some men no matter how bad the accident couldn't wait to get back in the fire house. That was how I felt, I missed my engine house. After going to the Medical Department in the morning they told me to go to my engine house. It took two months for my head to completely heal from the accident. I got to the engine house at about twelve o'clock or 1200 hours the crew was in the kitchen drinking coffee and talking. Lt Krolik looked at my head and said he thought they sent me back to early. We discussed the fire I got hurt in and the Engineer said they should of never used their water gun with us inside. It was too dangerous to take a chance with our lives, and just because it was new they couldn't wait to use it. One thing good about Lt Krolik, he wouldn't take chances with his men, in fact he was too cautious. It took me a while to learn that all the extra work I did helped me to be prepared for the fires that lay ahead. We had an extra man today because I came in later from Downtown, we had five men instead of four. FEO Greliski drove, FF Leroy and SFF Kalusey was one of the best, he would always go out his way to cook steaks for lunch. Thick ones at least a two inches thick, with fried mushrooms and onions, mashed potatoes, and fresh green beans. After lunch we all went to bed while Leroy took the watch. We were only sleep for a hour before we got a run. It was a four alarm fire on Grand River, the lights came on as the alert took off tapping out a four alarm fire on the register. The cook asked the Boss when he came downstairs did he want him to come. We knew that a four alarm fire was a big fire and that we would probably be there for a while. The Boss told him to stay and we jumped on the engine and took off. Our cook open the doors as we flew out with the sirens blaring at full blast, blowing the fog horn at every intersection. We sped down Grand River you could hear the engine rev and blow smoke and spill water everywhere. Leroy pointed out the smoke in the sky as we put on out gear. When we got to the fire the

Chief gave the orders to our Boss and he told the FEO where to hook up our Engine. It was a large abandoned Apartment Building , about four stories high, we hooked up on the west end around the side. I was told to stretch the line in through a side door. While I was pulling the line to the door I saw a friend of mine from Engine 42 FF Holmes. He grabbed the line and helped me stretch it. Abandoned buildings are very dangerous because they are old and run down property just waiting to injury us. We had to be very careful when we went in like Felton would always tell me. We pulled the line up the stairs in the double doors and around the corner to the vestibule. My partner Holmes was right behind me pulling the line. We had to find the fire on the third floor, we got enough line to take upstairs. When you pull line it takes at least 3 to 5 fire fighters to relay the line into position. One at the door, one at the corner, and one going up the stairs. That left me and Holmes pulling it up the stairs. When we got to the top of the stairs something made me stop, I had the pipe. Holmes said to me "let's go, come on, what's up, why you stopping?" and he was pushing me as he pulled more line up. When he bumped into me I stopped him, " hold up for a minute!" I told him, and we waited for a few minutes, right then the whole stairway collapsed. We watched it as it went right down in front of us, and we looked at each other as if we had walked through that doorway we would have been dead. We stayed there and opened our line because now we could see the fire.

We sprayed for hours until the Chief called us out. The building was too dangerous and was collapsing all around us, so we backed up and went outside to shoot water in from a distance. The Chief signaled everyone to come out of the building and fight it from the outside because it was becoming too unstable. We were there for about four hours until we were replaced by another crew. FF Holmes and I walked to the Coffee Van to get coffee and donuts from the Salvation Army Truck, that was at every four or five alarm fire. We talked about if we had stepped one step further what would of happen to us. We were very happy and did the black power hand shake before we were called to our Engines to leave. He asked me what made me stop, but I don't know something just stopped me a force. That was the first day I met Guardian Angels, and it won't be the last time I felt his presence. While riding back to the fire station I thought, what made me stop, was it just a feeling. Ever since I studied Psychology I wanted to have special powers, to know things before they happen. Was this me or was it another source working through me. Do I have a guardian angel? In my mind I felt the presence of two extraordinary beings, watching over us. Either I was a Bad-Ass _____ _____ or a powerful force is watching over my every moves. Has God finally made his move, is this his way of showing me he's real and alive. This was always in the back of my mind as I worked. Have I gained the superpowers of my dreams or God is real and using his power to not only help me but also revive my faith.

Dinner was ready when we got back to the station, the cook kept it warm. My fire clothes were wet, so I put them on the radiator. The steam heat would dry them and keep them hot, and ready for the next fire.

We were all tired from the fire and glad to be back at the Engine house. We had pork chops, rice, broccoli with cheese, and a salad for dinner. Fire house cooking was always the best they made sure that we had a good cook every day this was important. Without the proper food we would not be ready for the next fire. The boss talked about the fire at the table after we ate. We would always discussed the fire and tell stories. The Boss told us that when a structure gets weak, especially old buildings, we have to be very cautious, one of those walls could fall on you can kill you. After we ate I had to wash the dishes and everyone else was watching television or talking on the telephone. When I got finished I went to the running table in the apparatus room and looked out the front window at Grand River. We rested for about an hour. 1900 hours. Ring, the lights came on we got another box run. Tap.. Tap . . . . Tap came across the box this time was with Engine 42 on Livernois, we were the second engine. I ran to the radiator got my fire coat and boots, which were steaming hot. It's nothing better than putting on a hot coat and boots while going out in the cold. The Siren squealed as the front doors busted open we flew out blowing the fog horn, Honk .. Honk . . . HOOONNKK!!

We took Pinehurst to Fullerton spilling water all over the streets. I put my tank on and grabbed my axe as we rode Fullerton to Livernois. We made a left on Livernois throwing water to the curb, like we were on two wheels. I saw smoke and a fire as we pulled up to a repair garage with a big fence about eight feet tall. There were three big Doberman pinchers barking as we stood on the outside, Engine 42 and Ladder 21 was already there. One of the men from the ladder truck came out with a lock cutter and snapped the locks on the gate. The dogs flew out right pass us I was holding my axe ready to hit the dogs, but they just ran by. Engine 42 backed into the gate and stretched both beds. I put my axe back, and grabbed one of the inch and a half lines, then I went to the front of the bay doors while waiting for them to be charged. "We got water" yelled a fireman and I could see the lines fill up while other firemen kick apart the line. I walked to the garage doorway as some of the firemen worked on opening the garage doors. They got a door open so I went in there. It was so smoky I had to put on my mask, I could see only gray smoke, then I saw an orange glow. I tried to walk around some cars and a tool box in the building. I tripped and slipped as I got closer and closer to the fire. My face mask steamed up and my visibility was 20%. I had to pull it off to see, when I started choking I put it back on. I was hitting the fire when something came down and hit me in the face, then I could see. What ever hit me broke my face mask and now I could see. I was getting fresh oxygen. I got closer to the fire and finally put it out. Then I soaked the whole room with water, and made my way to the front to fog out the smoke. When I got to the front the other firemen were at the bay garage doors. Now they were open and I turned the hose on fog spray and pushed all the smoke out. Then I was gasping for air, because with the nozzle on fog spray it sucks all the smoke out right by you. If you put your lips close to the pipe you will get a little fresh air. My eyes were red and teary, snot running out my nose, my face wet, but I was happy to be breathing fresh air. It wasn't long before the smoke cleared and I could see everything. Its funny to see all the stuff I fell over and tripped on trying to get to the fire. Since we were second engine we were picked up after the fire was out. My company called me "Engine 49 time to go", so I gave the hose to someone else and left. I rode back to the Engine house with an awesome sense of accomplishment. I had a high that made me feel so good. This is what made me want to fight fires every hour of the day. When I was off I would carry my equipment in the back of my van, and when I saw a fire I would pull over put on my equipment and go in. There was a strength and power that came with this job. I should have though that it was God, but to tell the truth I thought it was me. I felt like a Super Fireman and that I could do anything. When I was at work I felt that no one at any fire could die, I would show up in the nick of time and save them. That was the case no one died when I was at a fire, before we got there they could but not when I was working, it happen just like that. I felt that I had the power to save Detroit.

The area I worked in became very important to me. I was working even when I was off. I had a responsibility to keep everyone safe, wherever I was at. I always wanted to have Super Powers where I could sense things before they happen. This is why I wanted to be an Astronaut, and when my dreams were killed, part of me died with them. This is what became of all my training, the things I have done as a child has lead to this career. Where I am fully equipped with practice I will prefect my skills. It is a real strong feeling of fulfillment that comes with working a job your good at and you love. I would work there without pay, I enjoyed working so much.

One day my old girlfriend Brenda told me that a boy down the street named Ricky took her money from her, and didn't give it back. She said that after asking him over and over he refused. I was with my brother D and some friends were hanging at the back of Hampton middle school. I hear about this boy who lived on my street. It just so happen that we were standing across the street from his house by the school's parking lot. I shouted at the top of my voice "Ricky is a Punk" ,"Anybody who would take advantage of a girl "Ain't Shit." Ricky's father came to the door with a double barrel shot gun and walked up to me. Everybody took off running but I stood my ground. My brother tried to move me but I wouldn't let him. His father said "why is everybody messing with my son, I'm tired of this Shit!" I said "your punk-ass son took money from my girlfriend and won't pay her back. Is this true

I going to get my son and we see." He went and got his son and asked him do you know this boy he said "no." Is this true that you took money from this girl, he said "no." His father got very angry and started cussing me out, he said I'm about to blow your ass away. I said "shoot me SHOOT ME"! His son was trying to stop his father, and my brother picked me up and started to carry me home right down the block. Ricky and his father was wrestling with the rifle. His father pushed him back raised the rifle up to shoot me. Ricky fell and grabbed his fathers leg and lost his balance. A shop rang out "POW" but I still refused to budge. When I thought I was right. I stood my ground. I have always been head strong when I think I'm right. I love trying to prove a point. This is another day I could have died but I didn't. Maybe God has been there all the time I just didn't notice.

My new adventures with the Fire Department has opened my eyes to what I was truly made for. I guess I should of thought it was all God, but I didn't. When I had my hopes of God and Jesus taken away from me, in a small room, in a dark basement with chants of "Jesus I love you" , and ministers pawing me until I would go into a mad fit talking in tongues. In a way it was what I wanted a visible sign from God, but what I came away with as the opposite. It never happen and I stayed in that basement for hours sweat dripping from my head. That was the day I lost my religion. They asked me on my way out if I felt better now, and I told them no, and ran off. I felt so bad like I had been tricked, I felt nothing different. Their promise to me was I would feel different. I WOULD FEEL THE PRESENT OF MY LORD. I do not. This is how I was tricked. They told me I could feel God, if I follow their instructions. I told them I don't need to feel God I am already one of his servants. We feel God's Holy Spirit everyday he helps us to live right, he empowers us to do God's will. They had me to believe that they had a gift they could give me. The great Tongues of Fire, like Peter going to Jerusalem, but my Oakland trip ended with me not getting the Spirit. My only conclusion was that I am not one of God's Chosen, and or He doesn't not exist. It was always something inside that I blamed Jesus personally because they used his name. I never let go of Him. Outwardly I never showed it or talked about it to anyone. There was some things I could not do that everyone else did. I still lived with what my mother taught me about God. I would never say that there was no God, but I thought it. I thought we just live and things just happen, and even though there is no God, I will still do his work for him. I was told by someone that God, and Jesus was just made up for us to be good. Since we were so abused as slaves we needed something to make us act better, and not kill the slave owners. I always Loved the concept of Jesus, and God and would live by His law even if there was no God. That was the way I was raised and I was never going to change. I just felt that God had no real powers. I tried to read the Bible and learn for myself, the truth. In that basement they stole my belief and I had to find out for myself what was the real truth. The Bible was so hard to understand, it was hard to even follow, but I would read it over and over. Then we only had the King James version and because of the language, the more I studied the better I would understand. I noticed a few things that people would use verses out of context to make a point, and back it up with the Bible. I noticed that a lot of people used the Bible wrong, making it say what it didn't mean. All this still didn't change my mind. My biggest problem with God was why would he talk to people in the past and not now. I asked God to speak to me at an early age. I have yet to hear from him. I felt that until He spoke he wasn't real in my book.

A friend of mine, Yah Yah was a Muslim and he said that his God and ours was the same. I got a Quran and studied it to see if that was true. His God was Called Allah and mine was Yahweh. There are people getting hurt, murdered, all kinds of abuses going on and where is He. Does He just allow all these things to happen? Now I have my turn to help and I'm going to do my best 24 hours, 7 days a week. In the Academy they told us we're always on call, that we never had a day off, if we saw something a Fire or rescue then we should handle it right away. This is what I believed and this was how I lived my life. Back at the fire station I couldn't wait for another fire, I would wash up get my equipment ready for the next alarm. I didn't care how my boss was treating me, sometime I wouldn't speak a word to anyone except to follow a order. I was silent and just waited till the next fire. We had a few more fires in the night, after them we went to bed and woke up in the morning. A day off was always nice they always went by so fast. The Bosses would always sit in the kitchen drinking coffee in the morning talking about the last day. I would just get my gear ready until my relief would show, and could I leave. I would be ready to leave to have a new adventure on the streets.

Yah-Yah was going to WCCC college at the time and he would bring women from school over all the time. He just brought three new girls for my birthday, Vicky, Poochy, and Bonnie. Bonnie was light and tall about six foot four, Poochy was brown and medium with a very nice body, Vicky was a star, light long brown hair with a body and a half. Yah took Vicky, D got with Poochy, and I was put in a spell by Bonnie. We just sat around and watched television, and talked, but we all hit it off nicely as friends. Being that Bonnie was so tall and thin and fine I was very taken with her, and she seemed impressed with me also. We spent many days together and had the three of us hanging out. We went to many parties, the park and downtown.

My next day at work was my favorite crew, Lt Maher was like Andy Griffin, FF Felton was Barney, McPhail was Goober, and I was Opie Taylor. Lt Maher was just like Andy, smart laid back, and experienced and a very nice guy. He knew the job and how to do it, he cared for his men you could tell. FF Felton was from the Vietnam era most of them came back with habits. If you had to do what they did most of their insides were torn , from killing not just kids but women too. I never knew what bones were in his closet but I do know how he treated me and other people. He was a stand up guy, he must have been a black panther or something because every time we passed a black man or some other black city worker up his fist would go up in the black power sign. When we were just riding he would climb on top of the ladder giving out the black power sign to everyone. It was like we are now in charge, we got these jobs and we're running the city. I hear some rumors that he used to fall asleep in his plate. One day he came in from the back smelling like burnt rope. When we worked together he was always there to help me right by my side. He would check out the fire when we got there and tell me what orders we had. He was my best teacher. I think when I came there to work he went out of his way to help me. He was like my older brother, in fact he reminded me of Rod. One day he did almost fall asleep in his plate, I keep on kicking him from under the table to wake him up. I thought he was just sleepy and, tired cause he started working on his day off cutting grass. FEO McPhail was one of the best drivers in the city, no one knew more or cared more about his rig than him. He was always working on the Engine or checking it out, even painting it. He was a country boy and he cared about his rig. If there was a problem he start at it early in the morning. He would fix it, or call the shop to do something about it. It was something about our Mack Pumper there weren't many of them, and they were special. Power, Speed and it could pump some water. I'm sure he was from the south, probably Kentucky , I vision him a moonshine driver running through the hills escaping from the cops. There wasn't a nicer guy, when he saw how good I put out the fires, we got along great. Not only could we beat them there but we would have them out before anyone else showed up, what a team. We got so good we began to take fires out of our district, he would steal them, and I would put them out. When the other rigs showed up they would be out and they would just help us clean up so we could go home.

One cold winter day our front doors broke and we had to open them by hand. The department didn't send anyone to fix them. All the fires or runs, we had to open them by hand and close them by hand. When we got out we had to throw a brick to keep the winter out. We still had the X-rig a old Keystone cop truck, with a running board this night. I used to love the Keystone cops comedies, the way they jumped on and off the fire trunks was cool. Now this truck is like a covered wagon, and riding the running board in the back was so much fun. It was the middle of the night when we got a run everyone, was sleep. I was on watch it was a box alarm, Ring, Ring, Ring, the lights came on as the box Tick Tick Tick, out 434. This was Schoolcraft and Meyers, I gave the address to the Boss as he jumped into the rig. Mc Phail jumped in and started up the rig, as it filled up the room with smoke. Felton jumped on the back end running board and hung off as I opened the doors. McPhail pulled on the apron and I closed the doors and threw a brick on them. When I turned around he started to take off , I ran to jump on the back but he hit into second gear too quick. Felton reached out to me and I almost caught his hand, but the rig took off to fast. I ran down Grand River as I slowed down, and they flew to Meyers and made a right. A man pulled over rolled his window down and asked me "do you want me to catch them." I said "yea" and jumped in and we took off right behind them. He was on his tail all the way, and when we got there the house was engulfed in flames. I said "thank you" as he dropped me off right in front of the house. By this time Lt Maher was getting out the cab and came around the back and yelled WHAT"S TAKING YOU SO LONG ABRAMS, GET IN THERE." I threw on my tank and jumped on the line. The fire was coming out the front of the porch, through the front windows. I kicked open the door and opened up my line. Felton had the second line and he hit it from the side. I stepped in hitting the ceiling first, in a curricular motion. I went from room to room first hitting the ceiling then the floor till all the fire was out. Engine 30 pulled up, and I was fogging it out. They helped us check the house out, to make sure it was all out. By that time Engine 42 and Engine 53 arrived we were finished.

I never told the Lt that they left me and he never knew. Just another hard day at Engine 49, Felton and I had a laugh about it later.

The worst night of the year was always the Devils Night weekend. This is every October 30 thru 31each year. The fire department receives an 80% jump in calls and fires. It started with just childish pranks. It escalated to the largest fire fighting catastrophe in the history of Detroit. Children used to dump trash cans, put soap on your car windows, throw toilet paper in your tree, throwing apples off the trees. It might have started with the dog poop in a bag of leaves set on fire when you step on it you get it all over your shoes. Then they started setting your garbage can on fire. One day it escalated to cars then to vacant houses. Since there were so many vacant homes after the riot. Many white families and businesses had moved out at an alarming fast rate. This was called white flight, and the suburbs were built. Many of the Detroit homes when they couldn't sell them they would abandon them. About half the homes in Detroit were now vacant. Detroit used to be a city that almost reached the population of two million at it's height, now under one million people. Fires spread from one end of the town to the other, only in Detroit and nowhere else. When I was younger we use to rake leaves together in a pile and burn them, in the fall around October. We used to burn our garbage in the back of the house but an ordinance was passed that stopped us for fire safety. Now in Detroit many people started moving from the city to avoid paying the tax. Then there were realtors telling them that blacks are moving into your area and if you don't sell soon your property will lose it's value.

The first freeway was the Davison which went from the eastside of Detroit to the west side. Then the John C Lodge Freeway was built which went from downtown to Southfield. It was said that it went right to John C Lodge's house in the suburb. Then the Chrysler freeway was built right through the most thriving black business area, Black Bottom, and Paradise Valley. Many Black Businesses and Churches were closed and moved because of this Freeway. The Businesses that were owned by blacks has never gotten over this move to retain their business economy in the city. The Freeways were built to the suburbs and most of the white population moved out of Detroit. That's when Detroit became a Black city and, Coleman A. Young was voted in as Mayor. There were a lot of people that didn't have the money to move out of the city, insurance and a fire could help them. If you had a property that you couldn't sell and you had insurance you could wait till Devils Night and torch it. All this made Devils night the worst night in fire fighting history. We would have fire after fire for the whole weekend, from devil's night eve till Halloween. It was Hell!

My first Devil's day at work, the beginning was a day just like all the others. I came in while unit one was leaving, their day wasn't that bad. They said they had a few fires like a regular day a couple of good ones at night, no big deal. I got my equipment ready and put it on the rig. It was a nice autumn day the leaves were turning colors and falling off the trees. My first day back the boss for the day was Lt. Kroilk. FEO Grenski , SFF Leroy, and I was on the back end. After greeting everyone I started cleaning the upstairs, dorm, offices, bedroom, locker room and mopped the stairs and cleaned main floor toilet. I liked to get the clean up done quickly. Then I helped the FEO mop the apparatus floor, and cleaned the office, dinning room and kitchen. Now I could watch television or read the paper, so I did both waiting for the day to begin. I sat outside on a bench in front of the fire station and watched people as they went by on their way, children playing as they went to school. Ring . . . Ring . . . Ring . . . The Alert went off all the lights came on as I jumped up and grabbed the phone. We got a dumpster fire in the alley down Grand River at Indiana behind the store. I gave the address to Lt Kroilk and put on my boots, coat and jumped on the rig. We flew out the door and right down the street, past Wyoming and slowed down and turned into the alley. There was a dumpster with smoke pouring out of it. The FEO pulled up close and parked. Lt Kroilk said get the high pressure line, this was a line with instant water, because the engine carries water in it. SFF Leroy handed me the high pressure line as I stretched it to the dumpster, pushed open the top, and opened the side. When the oxygen hit the smoke it turned into fire, and a blaze started climbing out. I opened the hose in the mouth of the fire as it turned to steam and smoke. Leroy got a pike pole and stirred the trash around as I sprayed the water in. The dumpster was put out quickly. Leroy went to the owner of the store to get the information. He said it was probably kids with matches. After cleaning up we took off down Grand River, Lt Kroilk opened the window and said we might as well go shopping now. Lt Kroilk liked to cook and shop we would go to different stores, as they would pick up things that they needed , from the hardware store and the grocery store. When we would go into stores with the Fire Engine Lt Kroilk would get a lot of free items. Fruit and Vegetables that were about to go bad, instead of throwing them away they would give them to us, so we would come back with boxes of food. Apples would mean I would be peeling the rest of the day and we would have one of Lt Kroilk's famous crumb top apple pies. That would be something to look forward to after a long wet fire. When we got back to the station Lt Kroilk made Polish sausage with potatoes and onions, and a salad for lunch, and apple pie for dessert. While sitting down for our lunch The alert went off again. Ring . . . Ring . . . Ring.. SFF Leroy ran to the phone I grabbed a piece of bread put in a sausage made me a quick sandwich while I ran to the engine putting on my equipment. I ate and got ready at the same time. Lt Kroilk opened the window and said another trash fire. This time it was in a field. I finished my food before we got there. It was just trash in a field so we used the HP line again just some leaves and trash, it was out quick. When we got back this time I ate very fast. This time I couldn't eat my whole lunch but I tried. It was very good. One of the best things at work were the different types of food from other cultures, the pie was excellent! We cleaned up afterward washed the dishes and mopped the floor. I usually stayed up but I heard it was going to be a long night. I went to bed 1330 hours. I had a beautiful dream about Karen and I running in a field when I was awakened by the alert, Ring Ring Ring. The lights came on and we got up put on our cloths and jumped down the pole. Leroy was on watch so I just put on my boots, coat helmet and slid right in my seat, as we flew out the front door, sirens yelling through the streets, honking the air horn down Grand River Avenue. It was now about 1500 hours and we had a fire in Engine 30's district. When we pulled up there were at least four or five engines, not including the ladder trucks and squad rigs. We had to come in from the back street because there were too many Engines and line on the fire street. Five houses were on fire one completely burned all the way down to ashes, all you could see was the basement foundation. They all were right next to each other. The one we went to was boarded up next to one on fire. We had to check to see if it was okay. Another fire fighter and I went in to check upstairs and two more checked the downstairs. This house was closed up tight. Boards on every window, so tight that it did not allow for any light to enter. I had my flashlight so that didn't matter. I had a super big flashlight, with a string tried on my arm so I couldn't lose it. On the way up I could see some smoke. The upstairs was an unfinished attic that had been framed and insulated but no drywall, so all the wall could not be detected. Now this made it hard for me to do my work cause we would feel around the rooms with our hands. The walls were just studs, insulation, and wires. I would go from the first room all the way around until we completed the search. The other fire fighter went the other way around. It was very hard to check without all the walls being completed. I was checking for fire and the room began to fill with smoke and the longer I looked the more smokier it got. Before I could finish, it was so filled with smoke the light refracted and nothing could be detected. The other fire fighter must have gone downstairs before me. By the time I got back to the stairway a blaze of flames and smoke filled the upstairs. I couldn't get downstairs. We were just checking their was no line with us, and it would probably take awhile to get one. I had to move away from the stairs, my only way of escape, and figure a way out. With all the windows boarded shut it was going to be hard. I had an axe, and right then my bell when off letting me know I only have 5-10 minutes to get out. I first looked for a window, but because it was locked up tight I couldn't find one. I laid on the floor and wondered what to do. Everything from the academy ran through my head. Was this it for me? This is what I wanted to do? My air ran out and I had to take off the mask, the room was filled with smoke. I got as close to the floor as I could to breath. When I couldn't think of anything else I took my axe and started to pound on the floor with it. BAM BAM BAM!!! Then I yelled "I'm stuck upstairs" then I banged on the floor as loud as I could. I heard someone say "someone's stuck upstairs." They got a ladder to opened a window. I got close my air was out. I was choking and coughing, snot was running out my nose but I was glad to see sun light and fresh air. Knock, bam they chopped and pried at the window like the Tinman at the door of The Wizard of Oz. Although I didn't want to alert them the way I did I had no choice. My pride had to suffer, me living another day, as I laid on the floor gasping for air. I crawled to the window as they chopped away. Soon the window was open. One thing about the Detroit fire department, when one of us is in any harm they will go though pure hell to rescue him, not matter what race or color! They tore off those boards like the HULK and they were on very good with extra support, reinforced with two by four's to make sure their would be no break—ins. When someone is working on a home in this kind of area, their might be some thieves that would want to steal equipment or supplies. The smoke poured out the window as they opened it, and I was right there ready to jump out as soon as the hole was big enough. He tore the last board off and I was out of there, in a second, fresh air we never know how precious air is until we need it and can't get it. I jumped on that ladder with FF Action Jackson a big robust strong black man, he climbed down first and I went after him. I couldn't think of seeing a better person, I was very happy to see him. It is so good to reach land after thinking that life was over for me. I walked back to my engine, as a few fire fighters came around to see if I was okay. I was fine now that I'm out of that house. I wondered what happened to the other fire fighter that went up with me? He must have came out a lot quicker than I, and by the time I got around to the stairs they were on fire. He should have checked the house out with me or said something to me before he left. Some fire fighters just hid and don't do any work. I've seen some hide in closets until the fire's out. I was a little upset at the FF that left me up their by myself, I almost lost my life. I was embarrassed to call for help but that's the way we work together no one can save a house all by himself, that's the best way to get hurt, or killed. The best thing about fire fighting that I love is that we work as a team. All it takes is one man not doing his doing his job and he can injury or kill another. After that I began to see other fire fighters that were not doing their job, hiding in closets, hiding from work, being there just to be paid. I worked for the love of the job fire fighting was my life. I ate, slept, and drank it everyday, working or not. I was glad to be alive but the truth was in my heart I would fight the best fight until I die. That was the fire that broke me down and made me think that one day I will die in a fire, but this is what I choose. My living changed, I started living a fuller wilder life on my days off. I still carried my fire fighting equipment everywhere I went but I stopped going in fires when was off.

I got to know my fire station neighbors on my day off I would stay in the area. I tried talking to some of the ladies around the station. I was introduced to a nice lady that lived right behind the station by FF Felton. I got her number but never set up a date with her. There was a cute girl that used to talk to me in the back of the alley, her name was Kim. She was real nice but I was just being friendly. A day later her mother came to the station to tell FEO McPhail that she was only 15 and I better not touch her. I wasn't really interested in her, we just spoke as friends. I learned that she had a huge crush on me that was what her mother said. We still spoke but I knew I couldn't do nothing with her. She was so shy that she would never say anything like she wanted to be with me. If she did like me I would have never know if her mother had not told the FEO. She was a friend of Freddy that lived down the street. Freddy knew everyone that lived around the station. As a child he used to visit the station and he knew all the bosses and fire fighters that worked there. He would go to the store for them and wash cars for money. He loved the fire department but was scared of fire. Long ago he had a got burned, and was saved by fire fighters. Freddy the fire buff introduced me to a lot of his friends that lived close. First was this fine brown skinned sister named Ivy. When she walked down the street everybody watched. She was a brick house, mighty, mighty she let it all hang out. Her walk was just like May West she acted like her, talked like her, and had her shape too. She was very sexy street smart girl, after meeting her we hit it off right away. FEO McPhail thought she was something else but Lt. Krolick, did not like her at all, although he liked Tony that worked for Edison. I liked her too, but she was always to busy or not interested in me. Just like a good father Lt Krolik wouldn't let Ivy visit he had his opinion about her, and he knew what he was talking about. I being young and naïve was just putty in her hands. Like May West my favorite star " why don't you come over and see me sometime" was all it took and she had me. We spend much time together and enjoyed each others company. For a time I was either at work or across the street with Ivy. It was easy to go to work because it wasn't farther than 50 feet away. I was a prisoner of love, and she was the mistress of torture. Now she didn't have to worry about me seeing another woman because she wouldn't let me out. That was the smartest way to keep me. Although she was so hot I could never keep up with her. She put me to work. I tried to satisfy her the best way I knew how, but nothing worked right with her. I guess she was too hot and I just couldn't take it, but I tried. She was very demanding and she always got her way. She worked at a Diner on Grand River and Schaefer, the truck drivers were crazy about her. I never though about marrying her but I was totally faithful to her. I enjoyed all the times we spend together.

When I was at the fire house Ivy would come to see me, I could tell she liked me. Lt Krolik didn't like her and told me she couldn't come over, he found a line in the rule book that stated I couldn't have habitual guest. One day he rode me hard he had me cleaning from sun up till sun down . No guest No visitors, and one thing after another, I was the only black guy that day, and they were having fun in the kitchen. I was pretty upset, he even told me no long phone calls, so at night we caught a fire. Ring . . . Ring . . . Ring . . . It was four alarm fire but it was out of our area, they called us as an extra engine. This fire was at a Funeral Home on Greenfield past Warren and it was blazing throughout, smoke and fire straight through the roof. I was on the 2 ½" line in the front with another black fire fighter. Shepard a friend of mine he always had a happy spirit, was behind me. I told him about the day and how the LT. was on my case all daylong. The fire when down and we went inside with an 2 ½ line, I was crawling around trying to get to the fire and I climbed into a casket. We started laughing I felt a little better, we put out the fire and it was about time they were getting ready to send us home. I looked up and saw Lt. Krolik with a 20 foot pike pole trying to break the windows on the second floor. I said there he is now. I looked at FF Shepard and said don't we need to fog out the smoke. He said yep and we laughed. I opened the line, the water surprised him, as he back peddled to get out the way. He then slipped and fell backwards as the water washed his face. My boss looked so much like W.C. Fields. We fell out laughing, threw down the line, and ran out the house. We were called to go back to our engines, I said goodbye to my friend and left. I went back and jumped on my engine when I saw the LT. he was dripping wet steaming mad, but he never said what happen. He went in looking for who was on that line but, it just laid there dripping. I smiled inside it didn't bother me no more, I just had to deal with whatever else he would throw my way. Now I will always have something that will make me laugh.

In the winter I got to know Ivy. She lived across the street from the fire station, Freddy tried to talk to her little sister. One day she asked me to come over to her house, she lived in the basement. It was a nice one with steam room, living room, bedroom, and kitchen, it was like a apartment. Ivy was a very demanding girl and it was hard to say no to her. She would usually get what she asks for. She didn't want me to leave for anything, everything was provided that I needed or wanted. It was nice I had nothing to worry about, I enjoyed myself. Time went by in her basement as we got to know each other, we did everything together. At that time I stopped seeing anyone else because I was always over there. It was a good change of pace instead of going out all the time. She took care of food entertainment and making love, I was so excited and she was so sexy it never lasted as long as she wanted it to, although I was very satisfied. She reminded me of my sister Denise very demanding, always getting her way. I enjoyed it as much as I could but being in a basement all the time I was getting stir crazy. I learned how to still see her while I was still at work. I came up with a routine. Since Lt Kroilck didn't allow me any company, I would work hard all day, make an excellent meal at night, then I would go to sleep early, on the cot. Then everyone would go to bed she would ring the phone one time and hang-up, I would then call her back. If everyone was asleep the coast was clear, I would put old oil buckets at the stairs and unscrew the light bulb. Then she would walk from across the street in her nightgown. I would open the back door, we would stay in the hose tower, I had a chair and that was all I needed, If we would catch a fire she would stay until we left. The fire door would open and she would walk across the street back home, in her nightwear. We never got caught and it went on for a while, but at that time she was so very hot I never could give her all she wanted and she wanted it all the time. I noticed a mean side to her but it was to everyone else first, then one day it turned on me. Our love making never lasted as long as she wanted. This time she was real mad. To tell the truth the more she pressured me the shorted it went. Maybe some people were never meant to be together. I thought I was a good lover but with her I was slipping, I never had to figure it out, it just came natural, but with her I had to use some new methods, like not paying attention to what I was doing, keeping my mind on something else, but with her it was always like the first time, she was just too exciting. She was the hottest I'd ever known just like May West, and everyone who saw her knew. It lasted all winter then I needed a change, maybe she felt the same since she was tired of me not satisfying her. One day I just got tired, and I moved on, but we still were friends. I guess Lt Krolik knew more than I about Love, but I would never admit. He was married and still happily enjoying his family life.

Then I met Freddy's best friend Steve, they grew up together, he was into making Hot Rods, and souping up cars. He first worked with me to tint my windows, Freddy would wash my car everyday I would work he didn't charge much a couple of dollars. Steve would bring me all kind of accessories for my van. I bought many different items to put it in my van, then everyday while I was there he would come over and help me work on it. When we got finished my van looked like a living room, with a pit sectional from Art Van furniture, speakers, sound system, mirrors, pillows, and it was comfortable. I was inspired by my cousin's conversion van from California. It became my passion pit of love, and I was on the move looking for love, all over the city. Steve started to go to Studio 54 Downtown on Friday nights. It was nice I been there before, but when I went with him it was different. He was a regular he knew the doorman, the owners, and the

DJ was Tyrone Bradley The Godfather of House. I got to know them, we would go to all his parties. Steve was a dancer too. We had a lot of fun there then Steve started a line dance where everyone would line up and we would dance going up and down the line. This was when New Wave just came out, and Le Chic "the freak" was being played. I would party every day I was off there was a party each day of the week at different clubs. We meet many women and we would go on many double dates, have loads of fun. We were going through women, meeting the finest in Detroit. I got many so numbers how could I call them all?

The schedule of on and off days made time fly by, fires, hang-out time, parties and new friends. The next day off it was back to the clubs again, Studio 54. This night I met a beautiful young lady named Angel and her cousin Tammy. I helped her put on her coat as she was leaving. I no longer needed to go out with friends, I started to go out by myself. She was a nice tall light skinned young lady with dark hair we became friends quickly. I hung out with her and her cousin Tammy a few days just going to parties and having fun. Everyday off was another party, and hang-out, I was always looking for ways to enjoy myself. Knowing that one day I might not make it out of a fire, was just a reality I lived with and accepted. Hanging out became a drug that I got hooked on, it would turn into hanging all night meeting new people, usually women, and not getting in until the early morning. I was late a few times to work and my boss Lt. Maher told me I could come in at night before I go to sleep. I started to come to work from 4am till 5am as long as I would make it to the fire station and go to bed then get up clean up and I would be on time. Other fire fighters used this tactic who had other problems that would stop them from making it in on time like drinking too much or doing drugs. I guess I fit in with all the other fire fighters, because no one was perfect doing a job like ours. Usually something was wrong with a person that would gladly go into a fire when everyone else was running out. The other fire fighters were glad that I was on time and I got to hang out as long as I wanted to, just don't go to sleep and make it back to the fire house before 6am, I was cool.

Ramona called me and we got together. I found out she was staying with another man at the time. I went to Cap's house in Highland Park, he was a singer in my brother's band. They all used to practice at his house, and hang out all day and night. There was Wyman the keyboard player, Amp another keyboard player, Clyde the guitar player, My brother Con III was the leader and bass player(we used to call him Conley Clark , like Stanley Clark because he used to play this solo that he did, he was so bad on the Bass), Duane another guitar player, Jan the drummer and our cousin, Jerry the singer, sometime Carmen another keyboard player and singer, different musicians would change from time to time, but this was the core. This day we were all sitting in the living room, I had a cold so I was drinking tea. I was telling them about a fire everyone was interested. My brother Con was not so amused. I was right into a tale when my brother said "calmly there is a fire in the kitchen," we all laughed, and he said again very easy "there is a fire in the kitchen." I said so "why don't you put it out," he said "because I'm not the fireman." I got up to go look in the kitchen and the tea kettle was bright red, the water ran out so now the kettle was on fire. I took it and threw it outside in the snow, it smoked up the living room, and my brother said again "I'm not the fireman." We all laughed ,and drank, it was the holidays so we had a good time. Cap had an extra room so Ramona and I stayed the night. She was always my girl, we caught up on times past. Ramona was my Angela Davis, I should of married her but I was to girl crazy, always looking for a better women. We had a wild night, I was making her hot toddies, that's brandy, honey, lemon, and we backed them with hot tea, well until I burnt the tea kettle. Making love to her was no chore it worked out fine every time, no complaints from her, and I was satisfied also. I couldn't understand why sex was so beautiful with one person and another was nothing. This was before I understood about the female organism well to tell the truth I will never figure that out. All I know is some I have no problems with them some I can work all night and into the morning and I'm just getting warm. It was a pleasure to be with my soul mate and not have to worry about anything. I guess that's why she was getting back with me, she had someone else but we were so good together. In the morning we found out why Cap didn't mind that we stayed in the spare bedroom. In fact he would let anyone use this room. Whoever stayed there the night before lefty us a surprise. This is when I found out that he let anybody use this room. That's why you should always remember what your mother says, always sleep on clean sheets. The first day back with Ramona and this, I was embarrassed, but we went through so much together. When we made love there were no questions or requests because we knew exactly what each other want we did it unreserved. She was my soul mate and even though we could not go on we could still get together, and make love like nothing else mattered. Maybe I wanted too much from women, that wasn't humanly possible, or just that after meeting Karen no one could ever take her place in my heart. It was Brenda my first love and I thought that she was the love of my life, but Karen by far out shined her. It was not just good looks, It was not that she was light skinned with long hair. Not even that when her hair shinned in the sun light it looked like gold. It was that she was beautiful on the inside as well as on the outside. She had a quiet side, and a wild side, she was a good girl, and a bad girl, she was smart and then sometimes dizzy. She was the only girl for me but she would not marry me. She knew me and loved me for who I was. Yes I was a Player, I went to bed with her girlfriends before her. I almost got with her sister before I met her. She knew it all about me and still wanted a relationship with me. I tried to replace her with every girl I met, but her image would never let me go. I went to northland with Ramona, we were in Hudson's my favorite place but I forgot one thing. This was my trapping spot. We were going up the escalator to the second floor. When I spotted another friend, Angie. I turned to leave and I saw yet another girl I was talking to Diane at the perfume counter. I looked at Ramona and told her I would meet her downstairs after I go look at some coats. When I went up stairs Karen worked in the children's department, then Elecia worked on the second clothing Department, I was talking to at least five different women that all worked in one store. I met Ramona in the basement and we left together , I knew that I could never bring another women to that store again. I don't understand why I had so many girls in one store, it must have been something about J L Hudson's at Northland. Brenda worked at the Hudson's downtown store. Was it the cloths or the style or that they were giving young beautiful women jobs. All I know was from that day on I never went shopping with a woman again.

Back at work Freddy and Steve came by to see what I was up to. Steve had a sister that wanted to meet me. Marshelle a nice small brown skinned young lady with long brown hair. She was a model and she just got a new house for rent and needed a roommate. All it took for me was a fine young lady like her to interest me, and it was real close to my station. I could now live in the neighborhood. This made getting to work easier, and the days off were fun to, she liked me but let me do what I wanted. Steve was there almost all the time, one day he went on a date and we got close. She asked me to keep it a secret from him so we never let him know. When he wasn't around we would have some real fun, we took baths together, and she would let me but didn't like having sex. If I wanted to she would stop me and say you know you really don't want me, and that she hadn't had sex in a long time. I could tell but that didn't stop me, we had some good times together just her and I in that house without sex even being involved. It wasn't all about sex with us we were real friends.

Steve would love to set me up on double dates. He enjoyed that I was around more now. He would always get the finest one of course. He was younger than I and he reminded me of my brother D. Being a double date partner wasn't bad. We met some nice ladies together. I didn't mind, some of those date turned out to be better than I ever though they would. Like Clarisse now she was a sleeper, light skinned tall brown hair but she had a lot of pimples. She was nice looking but didn't get much attention. She had a very strict father who I had to meet to get her out. Steve was talking to her friend who was superfine, and lived down the street. They could only go out if both of them went together. But as soon as we got them out we would split up. I was getting use to Steve always getting a Star. It didn't bother me I didn't always have to get the finest girl. Clarisse had some hidden qualities. We couldn't go home until the other ones were ready to go. I took her to a park and we would kiss but she was real strict and wouldn't let me do anything else. This went on for a while. When Steve broke up with his girl I stop seeing her. I went by and got her a few times because she was just that nice. She was a real nice girl and we had some fun, I should of keep on seeing her. Detroit was too full of beautiful women.

Then I meet Deidre another model, light brown skinned about 5'7", with a real nice body. She worked back and forth to Chicago, very business like young lady. I met her going out at a downtown club. We would dance all night into the day, she lived close to me. One day she came to visit me at work we had a new boss this day, Lt. Asbill. He was like Barney on the Andy Griffin show, but he had a nick name Crash Bill cause of a accident he had long ago. He was a very nice boss but I made a mistake of taking my new friend in the basement. We were just kissing but before long he came down to check on me, and ordered her out. Well that kind of killed that romance and because of embarrassment I didn't call her back, even though I saw her again I never set another date up. After that I learned to be very secret with my dates if they came to my job. I would sit in their cars in the front by the door so if we get a fire I could jump on and all my equipment would be there. They said we could have company but too many rules, and not to let them in my personal business.

I would only have company on the outside of the fire station, never on the inside again. Being a fire fighter attracted many women, knowing that's what I do has made it easier for me to sleep with them. Some wanted a real relationship and some just wanted to say they slept with a fire fighter. Many just wanted a man with a job. That was fine with me. I didn't always get who I wanted like the beautiful Karen who just wanted to have a good time. Maybe she knew I wasn't the settling type.

Lt Krolik only allowed me to see one girl at the fire station and she was Tony. We met her close to the station she was not just fine but very classy. She looked like Jayne Kennedy from the movie remake of Body and Soul. She worked for Edison when we stared dating. He knew that the other girls were no good for me. Like a good father he was right, but like a hard headed kid I had to learn for myself. She invited me to her house and seduced me in front of the fire place. This Beautiful young lady was as fine as a movie star, and I wanted a real relationship, but it never happen. I chased her for a while but that night in her living room kissing on the floor was the farthest I got. Maybe I should of given her an engagement ring but she told me to get her a sound system. Maybe I should of got both that would of sealed the deal. Was I cheap or not trying to be foolish. It is hard to tell if these Detroit women are playing games. I was such a romantic at an early age. I always claimed to have a more girl friends. It seems that I always missed out on the real love that I looked for. Now I just enjoy to be with beautiful woman. In this new line of work there is no telling when I might die. I will handle as many women as I can. This is what I lived by, I tried not to fall in love but, sometimes I could not help it. Love chooses who will fall and who will not, I was just a Player in the game. I wanted to be a Player for years, I thought I was the master of the game, in reality I was just getting Played.

My next work day was a regular day, I came in on time Lt Asbill was my boss today. I cleaned up the house like usual, got my fire equipment ready, and sat down to watch television. Freddy came by and asked if I wanted him to wash my Van, I said okay. Steve came by while he was washing my Van, I cleaned the inside while he washed the outside. Steve asked me if I wanted my windows tinted, it sounded good to me so I sent him to get the tint. I had a strange vision went I was watching and program in the station , of a man sitting in his car and smoke filling the car. I thought it was just a flash back from the show I was watching, but I didn't pay it any attention. Ring . . . Ring . . . Ring.. We got the alert, then the phone rang, Engine 49 you got a car fire at 11123 Manor, which was right behind the station. I handed the address to the boss and jumped on the rig, the cook was out so it was just me the boss and the FEO. When we arrived the car was filled with smoke, it was smoking from under the hood, pretty heavy. I took the High pressure line off and went to the drivers door to see if I could get the door open. No one came out to tell us anything so we just went to work. When I opened the door thick dark smoke came bellowing out before I tried to open the hood I had that flash of someone being in the car. I could not see anything so I just reached in and felt around, their was a body slumped over to the passenger side. I sat him up and pulled him out the vehicle by his shirt. He was not breathing at first but by the time I got him to the sidewalk he started coughing. He seemed okay so I left him with my boss and went to put out the fire. Now fire was coming from under the hood. The hood release was to hot it just pulled out in my hands. I ran to the engine and got a pike pole, (a long steel pry pole about 20pounds) I shoved it under the hood and tried to pried the hood open. That didn't work after working for a few minutes, I ran back to the Engine and got a axe. All the lines to open the hood must have been burned off so I started to chop with the pry side of the axe. I cut into the hood around the release latch in a circle, then I hit under the hood on the latch. When I got finished I used the pike pole to pry the hood up. When the hood opened fire broke out in a large flame. I then grabbed the High Pressure line and shot water into the engine, it put the fire out right away. The Boss called an EMS and they soon arrived.

They put the man on the truck and took him to the hospital. After the fire was totally out I cleaned up and we went back to the station. When I got back to the station I remembered the vision I had of the man in the car, it was strange to me, and I did not know what it meant.

Lt Asbill was a nice guy and I liked working with him, he was a straight forward person who knew what he was doing. We got along pretty well after I found out what he would go for and what he wouldn't. He wasn't looking for any trouble I think he had enough already he was just living out his day until retirement. The Officers who usually came here didn't have any pull, unless they loved fire fighting. One thing you would get from working at Engine 49 is experience and lots of it.

My brother Con knew that I used to play a saxophone in school so he let me know that a friend of his was selling one. I always had extra money so to me this sounded good, I always wanted to be a rock star. I made a pack with God when I was saved that if he made me a star that I would praise him with all my works. Well I never got that stardom I was always just an okay player if that. My first talent show we were laughed out of the try-outs. My brother Con told me if I would pay as much attention to my music as I do the women I'd be the best player ever. We went to look at the horn from one of his friends two cool white hippies named Ben, and Danello. We used to call Ben, Obie Wand Konbi from Star Wars a Jedi master. When I got there I saw the horn and it looked okay. They wanted three hundred for it so I gave it to him. Amp a friend of mine was interested in playing a horn so we went over to his brothers house. His brother had a straight neck soprano Sax, I had my new tenor and we jammed together. I showed him some of the basics but it's hard to blow a horn for the first time. It takes time to first blow a woodwind. Since I played from childhood Clarinet to Baritone came back to me. I also enjoyed playing that soprano. Amp tried to explain scales to me but they were too hard for me to understand. I just played by ear, although I knew how to read. After that I played all the time by myself to the radio I would just listen to Jazz and play along with it. One day I was sleeping after playing and I dreamed that I went to Bakers Keyboard lounge and Charlie the Bird Parker was on the stage and he asked me to come up and play with him. I jammed with him and his band we were playing "The Night in Tunisia," then I woke up and on the radio the song was playing. I thought that I was finally getting it, so I went to a rehearsal one day and jammed with my brothers band. They were playing and we hit a good groove and Duane the guitar player and I were going back and fourth trading riffs. My brother Con would still never let me play with them, and maybe I wasn't good enough. Then my brother got on me about carrying my horn with me everywhere I went. I would take it to belle Island and just play by the water. I had my horn taken to a shop to check it out and I was told the bell was real silver. It was appraised at $1800 dollars and this shop did some work on my keys. We got into it when he went in my van took my horn out and hid it. I still didn't listen to him and took my horn everywhere I went. There was a friend of my older brother Rod, Angelo the junkie, and he saw me at the fire station and asked me if I wanted to buy some tires for my van. He was going to sell me a set of mags for $300 dollars so I told him cool. We went on a ride to the East side by Van Dyke he asked for the money and pointed out the house. I pulled over and gave him the money, I never saw him again. My door on my van wouldn't close right because I used it to much, it ran off track. When Freddy was washing my van at the engine house Steve came by and was doing the tint on my windows. He saw that my door was broken so he asked me if I needed another. He brought me a door with a window in it and a painting on the outside, it was nice so I bought it. He hooked it up on my van and it worked good. I would always play my horn in the basement at work to pass the time. We got a fire after lunch right down the street behind the fire station, it was a van that had been stripped. While I was putting the fire out I noticed that it had the same painting and color on the van as the door just I bought. It was parked behind a vacant house and was probably stolen, I had no idea this was the case. Everything didn't come clear until we got back to the fire station and found out someone had broken into the fire house and took things like radios a small television. We looked all over to see what was missing. My horn in the basement was stolen. This hurt me deeply. I knew that the fire was set so that someone could break into the fire house, but I didn't know who. It all depends on who had the stolen van. I found out that Angelo had stolen the van. Steve got the door from him. I didn't think that Steve had anything to do with the break-in at the station.

I knew how low down Angelo was because when I was 15 and worked at a Gas Station he robbed the station I never told the police it was him because he was a friend of my older brother. I was street dumb. Most of the people that came to the fire station knew that we had money. I don't know if it was jealousy or just a dope addict trying to get a fix. Back in the day from my old neighborhood a lot of my brother's friend tried heroin. One day I was about ten years old and my older brother Rod asked me to come in the bathroom and help him. He had a spoon and something in it that he lit with a match. It melted and then he tided a rubber hose around his arm and asked me to hold it tight. He took a needle and sucked the stuff up in it, and shot it in his arm. He looked at me with a sad look on his face and said "don't ever do this, since I started I can't stop, but I don't want you to ever do this, Never mess with this stuff". He didn't have to tell me that again and I never saw him do it again. But he got in a lot of trouble afterwards. He broke into many places got caught and went to juvenile. He ran away from home many times. One day he came in and stole from my mothers purse, she caught him and they argued. She could tell he was high on something, he tried to hit her.

She took a chair and hit him over the head, it knocked him down but he was so high he didn't feel it. When my father came home he was very mad, he was no one you wanted to mess with. He beat him and the next thing we knew they sent him off to a Boys home. It was called

Hawthorne, then he went to Boys Republic reform school to try and help him, but they didn't work, they just taught him more dirty tricks. He used to tell us when he came home for a weekend. He learned how to cheat at cards and a lot of dirty jokes we would stay up all night talking went he visited. I loved my brother no matter how much he used to kick my ass, without him I would of never learn how to fight. To me it was all training. He was the reason I was so tuff. I just hoped that Steve and Freddy had nothing to do with the break in. I saw Fire Fighter Felton doing something stranger. He was falling asleep in his food. When we went to the fires he always worked and worked harder than many others. He was not like some of the others that would hide until the fire was over. Some at the station would drink beer and some would do other things, but when the bell went off they were all ready to fight the fires, and they did with complete accuracy. I not making an excuse the facts were they never got drunk they just had a few beers. When someone would have a problem then they would help them as much as they could. I seen men hurt because of a wife leaving them, and just like a brother they would do what ever they could to help during a stressful time in their life.

In my life since God was now dead, I made partying, drinking, and having sex with women my new God. After being tricked out of my religion, although I still had many of my Christian habits. Like helping the poor, weak and down trodden. I felt God was dead so there was no need to look for him. Now that God is dead who will do his work, now this fell on me. I still believed in good over bad, and worked on the side of good. With god dead this would be a hard thankless job. It was so hard to believe in something in which I had no proof. Maybe He was working in my life, I just couldn't see him. If I was to believe in Him, I just wanted a sign. One way to hear from god is to put him to the test. Are there special powers given to those who decide to do Gods work?

Chapter 6
THE BLAZE IS OVER!

THE EXPLOSIONS SLOWED DOWN, AND after eight hours the fire got to the point that we could attack it. The other fire fighters put all the other blazes out throughout the factory, and we were left there by the silo. The fire seemed if it would never die, but it slowly got smaller as the hours went by. Finally the blaze was controllable we shut down the 2 ½ inch Akron nozzle and advanced some 1 ½ lines into the warehouse factory. I shot water on everything that was hot, everything was destroyed. I saw the empty drums torn apart by the explosions, equipment scorched by the fire. After putting the fire out there was still fire fighters going through the building checking for hot spots, we were called to go home. I gave the hose to one of our relief and looked for Lt. Maher my boss, he was back at the engine. He told me that they were giving us another rig to go home in, because ours was still hooked up to the hydrant and being used. We left the fire in another fire engine, we were all wet and tired, but no one was hurt. All I wanted to do was take off these wet cloths and rest. When we got to the engine house I put my coat on the radiator to dry. The cook was there and our food was done we had a inch thick porterhouse steaks, with mash potatoes, green beans and a salad. I don't know what everyone else was thinking but I was ready to kiss the ground, because this day I could have been killed. While we were fighting the fire I thought that this was my last fire. It seemed if the fire was never going to go out, but we stayed there until it did. Many thoughts ran through my mind, I was happy and in awe of the power of fire.

This day I knew what God wanted me to do, fight fires and save lives. No matter how close I was to death I still wanted to do this work. I thought this was my last day on earth, but this was my most successful day on earth. If this was my last day, I have my father to thank for pushing me in this direction, after I though I would never do what I wanted to, he knew me best. My mother was always there supporting me in all my decisions, setting my schooling, any program she thought would help me. My brothers and sisters all helped me to become the man I am today. I lived a good life, and I thank God for everything he has given me. My true loves and my friends I thank God for everything. There was nothing more fulfilling than fighting fires, the feelings you would feel after a fire was put out was better than any drug ever made. I lived a good life, even though I never became an astronaut I loved this job. Fire fighting is what God intended for me. I enjoyed loving the beautiful women of Detroit, the nightlife partying every night till the early morning.

A radius of ten city blocks could of blown up property, peoples lives were at stake. The lessons that this fire has taught me and stayed with me all my life. One my life has purpose, two stick with it no matter how bad it seems, like that fire that I thought would never go out. My favorite boss Lt. Maher stuck there shouting out orders, not even trembling, not scared one bit, I got strengthen from his resolve. Just as in life we must stand up for what we want or we will forever be sad and beaten. This fire taught me a lot about this world how when you think you have lost and a higher power grants you success. At the time I thought it was me that had all the power, because at the time I wasn't believing in God all the way. I felt that Gods powers were limited, and that he needed me to do things he couldn't do, what a fool was I.

The lesson that I've learned was to always do your best, don't settle for less. Many times we may be beaten down, hurt, labeled a failure, and you may want to give up, but by giving up you lose. The choices made when one is hurt, in trouble, or feeling inadequate usually aren't the best decisions. Most of the crime we have is because there was one less opportunity to enter the career choice or job that complements a person. We can make this world better if we choose to, by striving for excellence. Words we say everyday are important, they have power to cause things to happen. We must choose wisely everyday what we say and do, because the reality of those decisions will shape your future. No one can change your life but you, where ever you are at in life, you are there because you allowed it. Many things may happen to us that we have no control of but what we do with these experiences can shape our life. It doesn't make sense to let a bad incident destroy our life, everything happens for a reason. I have found that by using those incidents to help others get through them can be the reason it happen to you. We all have instincts to survival, but many of us give up too quickly. From the very beginning I believed people when ever I was told I couldn't get in a certain career, I gave up. This was the bad decisions I made by giving up, and all I did afterwards to put problems in my life. There is nothing that you can run away from, because just like the planets go around in orbit, you will be right back in the same situation until you resolve it.

The Question that always stuck in my mind was, "am I following the right path." My direction was routed in the way I would run the football to the touchdown in a game. Hit the hole with quickness and power while looking for the next opening. My first quest was to be a professional football player that was met with a strong opposition. Then I was ejected from the United States Air force because I wanted to become a Astronaut. I told God in a prayer early in life if I was given talent I would praise him in my works. Then after being passed over when I tried to join the school choir at Higginbotham. I hoped my musical skills would improve but my woodwind, and guitar playing wasn't progressing. All I could do was make people laugh at me unintentionally for just being myself. I asked God to speak to me like others in the past, but I heard nothing. If God was real why can't he speak? I didn't know it at the time but I was asking for trouble. God is reveled in the Bible not by looking for an audible voice just to answer whenever beckon. I had no idea what I had done, God remembers every promise. I was told that by giving your life to God he would direct your path. What does this mean? He knows what I want when I don't even know what I want. The truth is He has a better plan than I could of ever know, by just giving my life to Him.

I went on to find my best path for a life career, after hitting many dead ends. Then I used my head to bust through some brick walls. I found out the best way to get God to speak to me was when I was so close to death before my time. At first I thought I was a bad-ass _____ _____ to cheat death so many times. Then it dawned on me that their was a higher power at work here. My eyes were opened when I was stopped from going into a stairwell by an angel. When I was stopped, my friend fire fighter Holmes asked me why I stopped. " I don't know, hold up" I said, then the staircase came tumbling down. Holmes asked me "What made you stop", "I don't know" I replied. This is when I started to see another realm of higher powers that consisted of Guardian Angels assigned to my life. Every time my life was at stake or pitted by the other firefighters I was protected. I began to pray for the firefighters lives, because I cared for them even though they chose to plot against me. This is when I noticed that there is a God. He knows me, and He cares for me. I was giving my life for others and this is something that God approves. Maybe my Lord was there even before that, I do recall other incidents where I could have been killed, and I lived. Was God with me all the time, I just never knew. In the Bible I states that God knows us even before we were born.

Crime is a money making institution so is the State or Government. Crime pays money for catching, prosecuting and housing them it is a business. To seek a better job or career for criminals might put some of theses people out of work. What is really holding us back from becoming a better world is people enjoying this reality now, not wanting to change to a better future. Profit could be holding us back instead of striving for excellence in every degree. All through time there were people that were enjoying good profits not wanting to change. When the new inventions of progress are proposed there will always be those that opposed them. That is why we must push forward to the best possible future that we can hope for excellence in every career choice. Everyone must try to be the best that they can. When one gives up, this can create problems not just for him, but others depending on him.

I have made some of my worst mistakes by giving up, and it has taken years to resolve them. If you have some desire in your heart "go for it" this is how you will receive your happiness. Let no one stop you from your quest, it's your life live it in the way you desire. An old saying I heard that makes sense "when you make your bed you will have to sleep in it" everything you do will have implications on your life. Make rules to follow that will help you, do what you know is right, and don't let no one guide your life but your creator.

What does God really wants from us? As a child I was taught about Jesus and the bible and what God wanted from me, but my question was why should I do what he wants when I can do what ever I want to. How does God know what I want, when I didn't even know it myself? It took me a life time to learn that what God has planned is far more than anything I ever could of thought of. I heard it said that to make God laugh, is to tell him your plans. My plans to become a Astronaut was a far cry to what he had planned for my life. To be a fire fighter was far more meaningful and fulfilling than anything that I had ever thought of. The search for happiness and fulfillment in ones life can elude many if you have no idea where to look for it. When I was young happiness came easy, as I got older, I had to try harder to find it. The simple natural ways to bliss stopped working when troubles and problems came. Man created ways to enjoy himself, with pleasures, having fun, drinking, smoking, and sex. It took a while but I learned that it was the simple natural ways to happiness that meant more then the fake ways. Like a new born baby, spending time with your children, teaching them, watching them grow is nothing more fulfilling than that. Being married and having a wife that cares about you, that tries to do what ever you want to please you, is true happiness and Love.

Chapter 7

DETAILS & TRANSFERS

AFTER RECEIVING MY BADGE AT Engine 49 and becoming a true fire fighter, the department gave me details to Ladder company 21 to get experience on the truck.(Detail is to be sent to another fire station to work for the day) I learned how to drive a tiller bucket there, that was for me another true loved position.(the tiller bucket is the steering wheel in back of the Ladder truck) It was something I enjoyed about having my own encased steering wheel on the back of the ladder truck. Riding in it was a thrill it made me feel like I was somebody special like my own space capsule. There is a lot of responsibility with this job. To turn the wheel in the wrong direction can not just only damage the truck but other cars and property also. The first time I drove in the tiller bucket was when we met Ladder 21 in a grocery store parking lot on Grand River and Oakman. That day I had fun and Lt Krolick was there to make sure I did it correctly. Thank God I never had an accident. I was very careful every time I drove in the tiller bucket. I had many trips to Engine 42 and Ladder 21 where I would be asked to cook, and was appreciated very much. There were more black fire fighters there, this is where I first met F.F. Watkins who later became one of the first black Chiefs of the Department of the Detroit Fire Department. I meet some other excellent fire fighters like FF Napoleon, F.F. Lipcomb, F.F. Hardiman, F.F. Lyons, and the Holmes Brothers twins, who I already knew from training, but only one brother could work at one time. They could never work together so they were split between unit one and unit two. They were on different shifts that was the rules family members were split up. There were many other fire fighters here because this was a Full House. That means a fire engine, a ladder truck, plus an EMS unit. FF Lipcomb who taught me how to make pepper steak. I finally got to meet older black fire fighters, and through their stories learned the wisdom of the Department, not just about the fire department but about life too. This is the fire house that F.F. Berry was sent to out of my academy class. His father was the Union president at this time. There was a Boss that didn't like me, and he was a good friend of Lt Krolik, his name was Lt Sarafinski he was the boss of the station. Lt Kroilck wanted Berry not me, so Lt Sarsfinski rode him about it and having the best TFF. Lt. Sarafinski was just like Krolik by the book always. They both ran a tight ship their crews knew them well and were very proficient. They were proud that they kept the traditions of the fire fighters. They were ready to send back anyone that could not match up. They would go back and forth on who had the best TFF. Most firemen would earn respect by the work that you did in the fires. I was known as a good and brave fire fighter that had never left a fire without putting it out first. Reputation was something that I worked hard for, something I learned in the academy that stuck with me.

One day at Engine 42 I was having a good time with the other black fire fighters, and the relation between black and white fire fighters at that house was okay. I was on the engine and we caught a fire about the middle of the day and we saw it before we left the station. This fire was going throughout a blaze from top to the bottom. It was right down the street on Stopel. The sun was shining bright. I jumped the rig and manned my gear. I was first on the line because I was the youngest man. (because of my age I was always youngest man and I liked it) When we arrived at the house, we backed up to the house, and I pulled the line off to get ready to attack the fire. I opened the bundle and grabbed the pipe while straightening out the line. I went to the side of the house, and entered through a doorway to the upstairs. While the other fire fighters went through the front on the first floor. I walked around the back, up the stairs to the second floor. When I got to the front door I kicked it open, then I put on my air mask. The fire came out the door with a roar. I opened up the nozzle and hit the mouth of the fire. I stepped in the first room while shooting the water around the ceiling in a circle. We fought the fire through the kitchen into to the living room. I just kept on going further from room to room all of them were on fire. That house was extremely hot, this fire was going throughout from top to bottom in every room. Other fire departments would not fight fires like we do in Detroit, they would have attacked it from the outside first, then they go in after it was out. My second man who backed me up on the line hit my shoulder and asked me if I heard someone screaming. I wasn't paying it any attention at the time, I was just working from room to room to get this fire out. When I thought about what he said, I didn't hear screaming.. Then I took another step into the fire, the water that was blown on the ceilings was falling back on me, now boiling water. Each drop of water that penetrated the crack between my gloves and my fire coat burned my wrist with hot scalding water. My arms were raised over my head swinging round in a circle to hit every corner of the room. All I thought about was putting this whole floor out, so I advanced further in to the mouth of the dragon. This is when I started screaming again, it was me that was hollering, and I didn't even know it. I tried to stop but the more that hot water fell on me the louder I screamed. I don't know what I was saying but if those preachers in that dark basement in LA could of heard me then they would of swore I was talking in tongues. All I was thinking about was putting this fire out, and when I got to the last room and the fire was out I went to the nearest window and fogged out the heat and smoke. When we put a fire out by hitting the ceiling first all it does is swirl the heat around like in a oven then add boiling hot steam to the mixture. This was a two family flat and the lower floor was going through out also like a double stacked oven both on High. Fogging it out a window will push the heat and smoke out of the house making it bearable. After we put it out the crew would check for hot spots. Then the clean up crew will breakdown the scene, then make sure the fire was completely out. Then we put all our equipment back on the rigs.

Needless to say I got burnt on this fire, so the next day I went down to medical. I would get two week or three weeks off to heal. When I would report to the Medical Department to be checked first, then I would go back to the station and my officer would check my burns to make sure they were healed before I could work again.

Details are when the manpower of each station are regulated to have a certain amount of workers on each fire vehicles. When stations are over or under the limit they will send different workers to houses where they are needed. This is determined by a schedule and a swing shift that will even out each house. This detail can send you anywhere in Detroit. It is good for new fire fighters to work in different engine houses. The Seniority system is set-up so that the person with the most time on will sometimes be needed to be a boss, when they are short. Each house has to have the right workers to run that house, because of the cut in men because of budget cuts, we all had to run short. An Engine needs a Engineer, a boss, and two fire fighters. A ladder truck needs a Engineer or a Driver, FFD, a boss and one fire fighter. If it has a tiller bucket then the fire fighter needs to know how to drive it. The squad needs a FFD a boss and two to three fire fighters that know how to use the equipment on the rig. The Chief needs a driver that could just be a fire fighter. A boss is a Sergeant, Lieutenant, or a Captain and sometimes a Senior Fire fighter could be a boss. An Engine has to have a least 4 men, a ladder 3 men, and a Squad 4 men they could have one more depending on the man power that day.

My day at Squad 4 on West Grand Boulevard at Mc Graw another detail, it was a hot summer day and my first time there. This was my first experience with the Squad and the Clown FF Best. We have worked at fires together before, I saw him but didn't know him well. I knew he was a very good hard working fire fighter but that was all. I saw another friend of mine a young black fire fighter but he was leaving for the day FF Small. This was known as a "white house" that mean not that many blacks worked there, or wanted to work there. The day started like any other day I got there and put my equipment on the Squad. FF Best showed me where. Then he asked me to make some Kool-aid and showed me where the sugar was, but the cabinet was booby-trapped. He had a string attached to a cup full of water on the inside. When I opened the cabinet the water splashed me in the face. This was very funny to the clowns and they laughed. The crew was white and I was the only black person working with them today. I laughed this was not the first time a trick was played on me, they told us about these kinds of tricks in the academy. F.F. Best found another way to talk me into opening that same cabinet again. "Could you get a pot to make soup out of the cabinet for me" he asked me. Splash right in the chest, another dose of water again. I can take a joke so I laughed, but now I'm on my guard. They tried the dirty toilet joke where he put peanut butter on the seat and told me to clean it up, while he stepped in to scoop some up on his finger and tasted it. He didn't know that I was a joker myself. I waited till he was on the phone and crept up behind him, and dumped a bucket of water right on top of his head slowly. He thought that was very funny. By the middle of the day the whole house except for the boss was dumping and throwing water on each other. We had the water hoses spraying water everywhere, we were all wet before the first fire. We ate lunch and had a few runs no real business; this squad loved fighting fires and without them they didn't know what to do so they played games all day. Squad 4 crew was what some would called a hotdog, that would run into any fire taking chances to stop it and save people as soon as possible. Like hotdogs they would get burned and hurt often, they would take more chances with their lives. I feel that you couldn't have a better crew of fire fighters they were just strange. After lunch I took a nap upstairs because you never know what was going to happen tonight so it's better to be prepared. We got a run while we were sleeping. This is when I noticed that someone put flour in my bed and my uniform was white with flour. They played games throughout the day. This was not my favorite fire house to visit. Good thing it was the middle of the summer and ninety degrees out. After then they just got on my nerves with the silly games. I tried not going there if I could, but many days I was stuck there for 24 hours.

We got a run and they said it was a child in the house. The dispatch operator would let us know on the way the particulars through the radio. It's the squads job to search and rescue so when we got there we ran in before they got water and searched the house. We ran in the house and made search of every room. We couldn't find her anywhere, then FF Best went to the bathroom. He reaching in the tub and pulled out a little girl. By the time I got to the bathroom, they were taking this little girl downstairs and to the Squad. She thought that if she ran the bath full of water she would not get burned. The problem was that in most fires it's not the fire that kills you the smoke does. Well this young girl ran the water, and was sitting in it apparently because that's where we found her down in the bottom of the tub. We don't know if she choked or drown but she was unresponsive, as she laid limp in the tub. She must have been choking because she kept coming up for air and was getting smoke. You see air is low on the floor not up high. The bathtub is not a place to hide. Every time she tried to get air she got smoke she ended up drowning in the tub. Every family should have a talk with their children and make a fire plan. Where to go when something happens. Have fire drills like at school to teach their children good evacuation methods.

Well Squad 4 arrived in the nick of time, but she drowned. We still took her to the hospital in the squad. On the way there the Sergeant gave her a Cardiopulmonary Thump (that's when you take your fist and punch right down on the heart) this started her heart back working and she woke up and started spitting out water. He wasn't Jesus but he brought her back to life. We took her down to Detroit Receiving Hospital and she lived. I saw the life given back to this young girl that we knew was dead.

This is when I became a "Super Fireman," I learned that we had super powers to save peoples lives. We were taught all kinds of life saving techniques and if we used them correctly they work. From childhood I always wanted Superpowers and after learning about ESP in school I tried to push my will into bring those powers out. Strange things started to happen in and out of fire and I felt like I was a Super Fireman. First in fires I had the power to sense things; I don't know if it was a higher power working through me. All I know is things happen that weren't suppose to and I started believing in myself.

I saw death past not just from other people but from me also. Many times I've seen death but for some strange reason I was spared. This is when my head started swelling and I started to wear a Superman T-shirt with the big S under my uniform. I felt that in certain situation I could do anything, and that while I was on duty no one in my reach would die if I could help it. It worked as I said, for as long as I worked no one died on my watch. Now if someone passed before we got there that did happen a couple of times.

Like at Engine 57 on Burt road and Schoolcraft a man was working on the road, and he had the beams that would form the curbs. He carried this on his shoulder and he must have turned it out in the street. A car came by hit the rail and it twisted around his shoulder and broke his neck. I was in the station house cooking a pizza when someone knocked on the door. We ran outside to see if we could help but there was nothing we could do. Seeing the blood reminded me that I had a pizza inside cooking so I ran back inside and cut off the oven. FF Fuller worker at this station, he was in the academy with me, and FF Smout. I heard some tales about him. He was a big 6 foot 4 brown skinned fire fighter with inviting grin. He was the first fire fighter I knew wear braids to work and get away with it, they tried to make him take them out. FF Smout would test, and push the boundaries of the fire department rules. There was a tale that he had a problem with a racists white fire fighter. What I heard was that

FF Smout waited until this FF went to the bathroom and he open the door stepped on his pants and punched him. There were no witnesses because it happen in the bathroom. FF Smout ended up being fired after he got into other problems. He was a legend to many black fire fighters that were being abused because of our race.

FF Fuller and I were good friends we used to ride to the academy together with FF Brock. One day we took a trip to New Mexico to visit some of his relatives this is when I found out that he was married. His wife and son lived there and he was going to re-establish their relationship. I thought we were going on a trip for fun and excitement. It was beautiful, a long drive through the mountains, and he never said anything about a wife. I never saw the mountain ranges and how the sun lit them up with the exquisite clouds scenes so I drew many pictures of the mountains. After sightseeing we drove around as he showed me some of the main streets and how they ran.

My skills of picking up women was at it's peak and we met some nice young ladies after visiting the college campus, University of Phoenix. I found a black area not too far from there, and met a real nice black young lady with long light brown hair. She showed us all around the black businesses and hang-outs. Then I picked up a fine Spanish young lady, when we were on the way to Fullers Brother-in-law's house. Anita and I hit it off well; she was into everything, we were choosing up on the women together. She was hot and come to find out she was bi-sexual, I thought this was very interesting. I talked her into having sex with us, and Fuller wanted to go first. I guess I was a bad influence on Fuller, he was trying to be like me. Well something happened, and he fell in love with her. She was a fine Spanish young lady with long dark brown hair, about 5' 5" with a excellent shape, and had a real nice attitude. She had a tattoo of a lady named on her chest. She was a real gamer and we had a lot of fun together. Lester begged to let him be with her first. After Lester slept with her it was all over. When it was time for me to get with her he protested. He picked this time to fall in love, just that quick. We came all the way down for him to be with his wife and son. I thought she was my girl, I was the one that picked her up. I don't think he had been with a women in a long time. He picked this time now to fall for a stranger. I wasn't going to let this ruin our friendship. I had no idea what was going through his mind. He was weak, but I didn't get mad, it was no big deal to me. Although this did end up messing the whole trip apart.

It was my Players code that we never fought over women, always let the women pick. Anita wanted to be with both of us, but Lester didn't understand that being old school, he was just "sprung." She was a fine young lady out shining his intended. This young lady was just like me, just having fun. She wasn't looking for a husband, or to settle down. He had money and she was ready to spent it. They went to the drive-in and I had to cover for him when he came back late that night. The next day we were at his in-laws house having dinner. It was an excellent meal, shrimp and vegetables over rice but it was super hot. When Fuller came into the dining room I noticed large red marks on his neck. It was like she was trying to eat him alive, she must of turned his ass out. I never liked anyone biting on me. This is a way to claim your territory, stake your claim. Women know how to get what they want. I tried to stop him before anyone saw and tell him because he had his butterfly collar shirt wide open. Before I got to him his wife spotted the marks on his neck and started screaming. "What the fuck is that, where did you get that from, Hell No!" All the lies in the world will not cover up a passion mark. It was a messed up scene that cut our trip short. We went home early, but he stayed in touch with Anita. I think he was having what they called a mid-life crisis. One day he sent for her, and she came to Detroit to live with him. I guess it was all my fault I should have never let him get with her, it was my ride and I picked her up. She was a nice girl but a little too hot and too young for him. She was superfine and I guess I gave Fuller more credit and didn't know his weak condition having no control with young fine women. How could I talk I don't have any control myself. Fuller was older than I and he longed for the days of his past. I was in my twenties and he in his forties, this must of brought back many memories of his youth. When he was trying to do the right thing, feeling he had hidden came to the forefront. This set up a long period of mistakes for my friend. After coming back home he sent for her. When the opposite sex notices that you are head over heels for them, they take advantage of the situation. She knew at his age that he would do practically anything for her. By using her beauty and age she had him just where she wanted him. Game recognizes Game. Anita was a female "Player", that's why we got along so well. A Player knows that it is their world and sometimes can use this to their comfort, without caring for the fool in love. She lived with him for a while then she started to have friends come over while he was at work. One day while Fuller was at work one of her friends she met in Detroit, started stealing Fullers camera equipment and anything that was worth money. He passed it to his boys that were waiting in the hallway while she wasn't looking or out of the room. They emptied his home of most of the expensive items he owned. The fact was that she was just looking for fun, to take advantage of his feeling, and she wasn't in love with him. It wasn't long before she got put out. She called me for a ride to the airport. We spent the day together. She had to go in the morning. It might have taken long but I finally got with her. It was only for one night because she went back to Arizona to marry a black young service man. I guess I wasn't that attracted to her. When she went I never heard from her again.

Lester finally got himself together and went to get his wife and son and they moved up here to live with him.

I guess many people make mistakes when it comes to relationships. Many times we go for what we see and not what we need. As far as home break-ins this was regular in Detroit. This was not only happen to him. Anyone who live in Detroit that have to leave their homes for 24 hours at a time. When they come back they can find items missing. Especially if they don't have family that will be at their house. When I lived on Griggs almost every time I came home something else was gone. From televisions to radios anything that was worth money. One day I came home and heard that the house was robbed at gun point. My brother D and Yah-Yah were there. I heard an old bully Huckabuck set us up. They didn't get much because I wasn't there and they wanted money. Everyone knew me and thought that I had a lot of money, because of the way I lived. This was how it is, to live in Detroit and I was use to this, a city wild and rough like the wild wild west.

While in the city working I went on many details at other stations in Detroit. At Engine 59 located on Curtis and the Southfield Expressway we were called to a house where a man was sleeping with a cigarette. He probably dropped it in the mattress. What happens when you do that is a slow smoldering in mattress and couch stuffing a lot of flammable fibers, like hay and cotton. These kind of material fibers burn slowly, smoldering the fire for a long period of time. The fire will be undetectable, just smolder for hours like this one. It's the smoke that kills carbon dioxide slowly puts you in a dreamlike state while taking your life.

He just lived right across the street from the fire station, but it was still too late. Carbon dioxide is a fume that comes from the combustion. We were called too late, he laid in a fetal position he could have been dead a long time ago. The mattress never caught fire it just smoldered. The family was very upset with his death, he was an older man.

At Engine 44 on 7 mile and John R, I was stationed there on a detail and I ran into a old friend of the family FF Mills. I was working a relief for my friend FF TVChetham. I was on the engine this day. When we got a run to Gallagher street on the eastside by Nevada. We were the second engine, when we pulled on the side of the house and we went in through the back. There were two houses on fire side by side. As I walked up to the house my helmet fell off. When I reached down to pick it up a 220 electrical line buzzed by right past my head. I could feel the heat from it's spark as it went by. I don't know why my helmet fell off, I knew if it didn't I would have been dead on arrival that day. I was amazed that day although I didn't stop to marvel, I just kept on doing my job. After we put out the fire we talked about how lucky I was. We would all tell fire stories after the fire was out, helping us to learn about our experiences. I told about the time four flights of stairs collapsed with one of the Holmes brothers, and I was strangely stopped by a unknown force. That was the beginning of my near death tales.

Engine 30 on Meyers right off the John C Lodge Service Drive was a busy house like Engine 49. We worked on some of the same fires together. When I had a detail there, it was a very busy day working all day and into the night, fire after fire. This fire house was located next to the Phoenix, the Black Fire Fighters Association which I was a part of. I joined them and would come there and hang every now and then with the other black fire fighters. Theresa the only Black female fire fighter at the time worked there also. She lived around the corner from me, she was a brown skinned thick lady about 5'5, with a nice white smile. My problems were nothing to hers. When she went to work everything changed. Being the first female the officers had to make sure nothing wrong happened at the station. They worked hard to make her quit but she just kept on working until she got hurt in a fire.

Engine 53 on Fenkell and Greenfield was the Black Engine house where some of the first black bosses were located. There was Sergeant Neal, he was the coolest guy I ever met. Tall, thin like Marvin Gaye and his crew felt that they were the best. They had tried to steal fires from us many times. They had their basement fixed up like a hangout, with a color television, posters on the walls, it was real nice. They were a bunch of braggers and boasted that they were the best in the district. This is how they would fight fires, by running through a house and knocking down all the flames then they would jump out the window throw the lines down. Then they would start smoking and sit in front and brag about how good they were. We would still be inside working, checking for hot spots looking which way the fire ran, accessing the damage, how it started, then cleaning up, and putting away our equipment. I liked them all, it was good to see a station almost full of black fire fighters. I will admit they had the best location for beautiful women at this corner, sitting outside would guarantee me a least two or three good phone numbers each day.

Now at Engine 51 on Livernois at Curtis this was my dream station but this was a very important station, because of the homes that they protected. This was the first time that I saw real care given to the home owners. Many of these home were very expensive right behind Palmer Woods. There are many mansions in Sherwood Forrest also some of Detroit most exclusive homes. Yes this was my neighborhood where I wanted to start working. The first fire house I ever saw, before I started working. We had a fire on Birchcrest a large mini mansion corner house with a huge front door. When we arrived the owner met us at the door and took us to the fire. I was told "don't think about breaking windows, open them if need be," by my boss. The carpet was a deep white shag. We walked in and went upstairs, it was very smoky so I opened as many windows as I could. We got the fire out quickly and helped the owner clean up the mess. The care that they would give I had never seen in the department. There weren't many fires in this area because most of the homes were occupied and worth lots of money. On the eastside this house would have at least 20 windows busted by now.

It depends where the house is located on the type of care that is taken. Palmer Woods and Sherwood Forest has the best service because of Engine 51 and the caring fire fighters there.

I was transferred to Engine 18 to work on the Ladder Truck and get my experience with rescue and ladder operations. This station was located off Gratiot on the eastside. I met one Wild E. Coyote on the first day, his name was FF Wiley, who was a real character. He would start his day off at the television laughing and talking to a Cartoon preferably the Road Runner. I first saw him screaming in the kitchen "watch out road runner he's gonna catch you, uh oh you better run, ah ha ha ha" he was standing in front of the television talking to it. Now if he wasn't crazy I don't know who is. He was an experienced Truck man, and was on the job a month longer than I. In fact we were in same class until I was taken out for not passing the physical. We hit it off real well, and I found out that he was Wilder than I could ever be. He got along with everyone, all the officers there was no black and white problems at this station. He showed me the ropes on the roofs, and this job of being a trunk man which I grew to I love. I learned how to put holes in the roof, put up water towers, and all ladder operations. When there was a fire it was our job to do the ventilation, that means opening windows and holes in the roof. A truck man does most of the clean up work. We use the pike pole to pull ceiling down and check for hot spots.

One day I ran into a little problem with another fire fighter I dropped my pike pole and it went right by his face. He got mad and wanted to fight at the fire but I wasn't paying him any attention. He got in my face hollering but I stood my ground. I apologized but that wasn't good enough for him he wanted to fight. He insisted I did it on purpose. I really don't know the real reason why he wanted to fight. What I couldn't understand was that he was black, on the Westside we all got along. I heard that he still tried to start things, and at every fire he acted like he had a chip on his shoulder but I wasn't going to fight him. He would send rumors around talking about me, but I never let him get to me. FF Wiley and I became very good friends and I found out that he was more crazy about women than I. He would try to talk to every women he would see. I would pick them on the looks, and style. He didn't care as long as they were female it was okay with him. This reminded me of and good friend in school, Chucky he would ask any girl for her number, yes you would get turned down plenty, but you would also get numbers you never thought possible. We would stop women all day by standing in the doorway flagging them over and inviting them in. It was a contest to see who could get who, he would always win cause he was quicker than I. We played basketball together and one day I was bragging about running track, and he called me out. We ran a race down Mt Elliot about 100 yards and he beat me, he was real fast. We had a couple of young ladies in front of the station, one day and one of them was taking potatoes. She invited me over one night, and this is when I first noticed the different between the Eastside girls, and Westside ones. She was like a wild cat, and she almost scratched my back up. I had to hold her hands. When I turned the lights on I saw a million roaches on the floor and they all scattered. I had to hang my cloths up so they would not get in them. Now I understood that there was a lot of poor Detroiters that came to the station because they knew we had good jobs. I had to up my game if I was too slow he would of gotten the number already. I thought that I was the ladies man but he showed me up many times over, but it was cool. Wiley and I would go everywhere he introduced me to all the cool fire fighters black and white. Everybody knew that he was crazy but they all liked him. He had many friends I never saw him have a problem with anyone. We would hang out on Mt Elliot Street down from the station, after we got off work and tell stories before we went home. We had an excellent cook FF Ryan a cool hippie type that would cook on the grill almost everyday. They had an outside gas grill that they hooked up. One day he made these short end ribs that were so good, and made so many we ate them all day. I ate so much that night I got sick. At 4am I had to get out of the bed, run to the bathroom and vomit. I was such a pig, they were so good, I couldn't stop eating them.

Swing Detail

Now I got to work at all the eastside fire stations and meet all the east side fire fighters. Ladder 16 was a detail from Engine 18 it was located on Miller Street right under Van Dyke, a kind of secluded station in the middle of nowhere. I sat on the street in the ticket booth selling fireman field day tickets all day. At this time the Detroit Firemen field day was a big deal. The Fireman's fund would raffle off twenty five brand new high end cars, and everyone in Detroit would buy the tickets because they helped the widows and disabled firemen hurt in the line of duty. My good friend FF Wilkinson was the top salesman.

It was a good tool when meeting young ladies. There was some nice young ladies in the area. I met a group of wild redheads on St Cyril street. Who came by and visited me a few times. There was a girl that lived down the street that would come visit me but she was too young, I don't know why I always attracted young girls. I stayed friends just to talk it was nice to have company. We just talked to pass the day away. I was so young that all the other firemen were at least ten years older than I. I enjoyed meeting the people that lived around the fire house.

One day I met one of the first black Sergeant's daughters at a party. I didn't know that she was his daughter and she was real nice and spoiled. When I found out I never let him know because I didn't want any problems. She was nice, we dated, but nothing ever became of it. She was too spoiled for me good thing she went to college right after I met her.

Engine 46 on Mt Elliot by 6 mile was an okay engine house. This was a medium speed engine house with only a few fires each day. It ran with a truck so their were eight men working there. This station played cards for everything, who washed the dishes, what watch you would be on, and then they played them all night long. I liked this because this day I got a winning streak that lasted all day. First I didn't have to wash a dish, then I won the watch so I could have gone to sleep, but I stayed up and played cards all day long. This was fun, it made the time go by fast; when the night came they started to play for money. We ended up playing all night long. We had some fires in between but when we got back and cleaned up we played again. When I left that station I had won one hundred and eighty dollars, I never counted on that, I was just playing for fun. One guy owed me more but I let him go and never asked for it. I know he was glad he didn't have to see me again.

A lot of my girlfriends went to college and when my sister did I ended up visiting them. I would take her up to Hampton University in Virginia in my van. It was nice there with so many beautiful ladies. My sister had some real nice girlfriends like Philly that I fell in love with just from sight. I wanted to go to college but the fire department was better suited for me. First I wasn't ready to do my studies secondly I might of flunked out. I did go to WCCC the community college and I wasn't that interested. I had a friend that went to Western Michigan college and when he got out he joined the Police department, Martin. We grew up together. When I was ten, he gave me his paper route when they moved. I am four years ahead of him because I started the fire department at eighteen. He went to Western Michigan to get his degree, then he became a police officer.

By visiting the colleges I was seeing what I missed. If I had gone to college I could of joined NASSA like I wanted. Although I was glad that I was fire fighter this, was the best life for me. Being a spaceman is just running away from the world, while fighting fires is helping to save the world. It was good to visit all of my friends who went to college and meet new ones there also. I even stopped at Karen's college on the way home from dropping off my sister. I also went to another black college and met some other ladies from Detroit. I asked Karen to marry me and she told me no before she went to school, but we still stayed cool. I used to talk to most of her friends, so why should she. I guess she was smart by not marrying me, she saw the painting on the wall. First it was Pat, I was crazy about her sister Cynthia before I even met her. I met Brenda first then I was dating their friend Audrey. After I stopped talking to Karen, I used to hang with Pat her cousin. I must have been crazy to even think she would marry me. I was just in love and she was so fine. I think she was one of the most beautiful and intelligent young ladies that I ever talked to. It was hard to ever match her style. It seems like I tried all my life but could never find anyone that could compare to her.

Except for Elecia, a childhood friend that I ran into after she grew up, we had an excellent relationship. I was in Love again. She was going to Wayne State University and I would take her back and forth to school. She was light skinned with curly light brown hair and green eyes, she looked like Little Orphan Annie. I knew her brothers they were the paperboys when I was very little. They used to ride us on their bikes, they were Jamaican. She had a very nice mother with a thick Jamaican accent, she looked like my mother light with green eyes. Early in the morning on the way to school she was just like my sister. She had a mean streak a mile wide and she wouldn't take any shit. She was very smart and taught me a lot, about women. She was real similar to my sister, very demanding, but I liked it.

When I would take her to school in the mornings I never met a meaner girl but in the evening she was the sweetest young lady. Now she was just as fine as Karen with a Jamaican twist. My heart will always love her. We stayed friends and she was one of the girls that was working at Hudson's Department store. She knew about Karen they went to school together, Cass Tech. She found out that I wanted her and told me " you should try to get her because that's where your heart is." She was a real lady with class and we had a lot of fun.

Chapter 8

MY TRANSFER FROM ENGINE 49

MY FATHER STILL WANTED ME to go to college. The commissioner transferred me to Engine 30 because it was close to Marygrove college. I did take some classes at the Northwest Activity center. Wayne State University was sponsoring courses there. I took a few but my attention was very low. Now I knew that I would of flunked out if I went to college first. It must have been the action that interested me. Working in a factory was boring. Sitting in a classroom of a subject that I had no interest in wasn't working.

The transfer got me another enemy. When I was shipped in I pushed another fire fighter out of engine 30. He was very mad, and he spoke of this when he talked to many fire fighters. He blamed me for him getting kicked out. I don't understand why I other black fire fighters could get to hate me. I thought that I would get into a fight with a white fire fighter. That never happen, only my own race found problems with me.

After I was transferred to Engine 30 it wasn't long when I was transferred to Engine 57. The seniority system made sure that all the young fire fighters would be in houses that no one wanted. Most of them laid at the outskirts of the city. Outpost is what they should have been called. Most of them sat alone, single engine companies with slow incidents. Many days would go by without a fire. Engine 57 was a peaceful station close to River Rouge park.

This is where I found true love and one of the worst fires of my life. Down the street from the Fire Station I heard there was a fine young lady named Starlette. I would sit outside to see her because I heard of the tales of how fine she was. One day I met a skinny light skinned young lady named Trula. She would stop a talk to me on the bench for a while. I found out she was the younger sister of Starlette. While she visited I found myself liking her, in fact I thought she was finer than her sister. Although she had a boyfriend, we became friends we would talk for long periods of time. Before long I was helping her back and forth to school and anywhere else she wanted to go. I tried to kiss her and to get closer but she stood her grounds and didn't let me. We were real friends and stayed that way for a long time. I stopped trying to get with her. I respected her, and still helped her back and forth from school. I did a lot to help her, giving money, let her use my van if she needed, and never expected anything from her.

Jesse and I would go to many high schools picking up girls, we would just sit on the outside and wait till they got out. We would go from Cass, to Mumford, but his favorite school was this Catholic all girls school, Immaculata, how could we lose at a school with nothing but girls. I snuck in the school one day with my friend Ziggy. I had the time of my life nothing but girls all around. Like when Jerry Lewis was stuck in a all girl school with Dean Martin. I just went to the girls bathroom and met some of her friends. I got out before the nun caught me.

Jesses just transferred from U of D to go to Renaissance High. One day while picking up Jesse from Renaissance High school I met the dream of my life, a young 5' 5" five brown skinned beauty, Cassandra. We hit it off and the days melted away as I fell in Love again. When she would hug me I never felt better, it was a feeling of total bliss. We were so tight that we were talking about marriage. She told me that she wanted to get married to me. I agreed and was happy. Trula would drop me off at her house, and pick me up later when she needed to use my van. I told Trula how in love I was, and that we planned to get married. She had a boyfriend and now I have a girlfriend. I thought things worked out pretty well. She was happy for me or at least she told me that she was. Then one day Trula told me that she wanted me, and she gave in to me. I was confused I wanted Cassandra but I also wanted Trula.

Trula took her time she didn't try to stop my relationship with Cassandra, but she gave me all the love I wanted. It wasn't long before Cassandra knew what was going on. She didn't believe that Trula and I were just friends. I let Cassandra go slowly but this hurt me deeply, because I did want to get married to her. Cassandra told me if I wanted her I better straighten up, and pay her more attention. I didn't and I lost her, but I had Trula who I wanted for a long time. It was good for a long time but I think we started off on the wrong foot.

A good woman knows what to do to get her man. Trula was too nice and let me get away with everything. She was always there for me not just as a friend, can I say I wasn't use to getting what I wanted. All is fair in Love and War.

I thought that marrying Trula would be a breeze. She could iron my clothes everyday so I would have a clean uniform to wear to work. When I would come home from work my breakfast would be done, when the night come dinner. She would be a good mother to my children. We would make love all the time, anytime I wanted, many times when I didn't. She wanted it all the time, I for once I could not keep up. No matter what we argued about we always went to bed together. These are all the things anyone would need in a marriage. I had only one problem no chase. All I ever wanted I had. The problem was no chaos, no craziness, no dragons, no rescues, what is a shinning knight in armor suppose to do. Boredom entered and my mind wandered. I felt smothered like I couldn't breath at times. Yes I like hugging but something deep down inside disturbed me. A feeling of restlessness. We broke up and got back together many times, but I didn't appreciate her as much as I should of. If I had the worst wife in the world first, maybe I would of appreciate the best. Through it all we stayed friends and never had any real fights, but she wasn't going to take just anything I was putting out. She was just a woman who I couldn't say no to, maybe there were others. That could be my problem, it's real hard for me to say no to any beautiful women. This might be a problem for many men, the women have all the power, and when it's time how many men can say no to a desirable women. Someone that you want to love asks you to make love to them. I have always felt that by saying no you invoke some kind of gay instinct. I have had women that I wasn't attracted to call me gay because I would not sleep with them. Anytime I would not let a women have her way with me, they were not interested anymore. I was the opposite when I was turned down I would work harder to be with them. Like the time I met Darnetta a beautiful tall dark young lady with the most shapely body. She had a twin sister too that was just as fine as her. After meeting her she asked me come over. She lived in Highland Park. I was very attracted to her but when I visited her for the first time in my life I said "no." When I went by to see her at her house she was all over me. Yes I enjoyed her passes and I wanted to do something with her but this time I didn't. We stayed friends for a long time but after that she lost her interest in me. Women love that control they have over men, so why deal with someone who can resist them.

This is the way our American society is made women says no and the man says yes. Every movie that I saw where the man turns down a beautiful woman it discusses me. To me it doesn't seem real, unless he has a better one at home. After all the women I've known, and trying to become a Class A Player, I think there is no coming back from one of my major influences Dean Martin, as Mat Helm, my role model. Television and movies had too much control over my life I had not even realize. Now I obtained it, I can never live a normal life. Maybe this is a normal life to be single and looking for that perfect women. Then after finding that perfect lady to lose her.

There has to be a special lady for me, one who can understand who I am, and what I'm here to do. Being a special man there must be a special woman to complete me. It took me a long time to understand that I was made to do a certain task and until I have completed this task I will not be truly happy, not even true love. It's something on the inside that has to be satisfied, and if not I will always seek it. The many women I've had were just my way of escaping the hurt of a broken heart, or trying to. When it's come to women no plan has worked yet, trying to learn love from the street is the worst plan. I would subconsciously find a way to end any meaningful relationship before my heart could get use to them, because I was afraid of commitment. Her words were still in my mind. This has worked very well for me from Kathy until now, even with her ever wise advice. "There are more fish in the ocean" which still echoes in my mind. Which means if it doesn't work out keep trying. One day you will meet the right woman. How I have tried to become a regular man and live a normal life, I failed every time. It was not meant for me, I have a different fate, and I must submit my will to the cause.

The worst fires of my life has always happened at the slowest engine houses. Starting at a fast running engine house kept me in practice. Learning everyday with new fires, one right after another. Slow houses are different, after sitting all day for weeks with no fires to fight. The rigs are sitting too and moving parts do rust without motion. The equipment could be old and not in a good working condition. The crew could be escaping from work by transferring to a slow house. Whatever the reason slow houses were dangerous to my health.

On a regular day at Engine 57, in a simple house fire right down the street on Evergreen, in a government housing complex, townhouses that were built with cinderblocks. We received the call as a house fire, I manned the rig like any other time, and rode the engine as the siren squealed and the fog horn alerted the area of our arrival. We took Schoolcraft to Evergreen splashing water all the way when we arrived, the fire was just on the first floor. The blaze pushed through the living room window. It didn't seem to be a bad fire, after pulling the bundle off and dragging it to the front door. I opened it and took the pipe out. I spread out the line and waited for water. When I got water I put on my mask and enter the house with the hose wide open. When I stepped in I hit the fire like an expert which I was at this time. I hit the ceiling with a circular motion until it was all out. It was like stepping in an oven, it was hot but there was no screaming this time. I was in there for a while yes it was hot but my experience lead me on. After I put the fire out I fogged it out. It was real hot in there like stepping into an oven. We got the fire out and cleaned up I came out to check my arms because they were still burning. I took my fire coat off and saw that my arms were burnt. The steam from the fire went up my sleeves and burned my arms. At the time I didn't know how bad it was, I was use to getting burned it came with the territory. I was taught to stick with a fire until it was put out, yes it was hot but I never gave in to any fire. I considered myself to be the best at what I do. Yes I was gung hoe and proud of it. This time was different, this burn was more severe than I thought. I have had many burns to my wrist, because of my body style my arms are longer than the coat. When I handle the pipe I raise them over my head extending my reach. The coat sleeves will naturally fall down because of gravity. The department did start using longer gloves that would come down over our wrist. It was the heat in that fire was too intense no matter who fought that fire they were getting burned. My skin was all winkled from the top of my wrist to the bottom of my forearm, my face and neck was burned also. I was taken to the nearest hospital Northwestern, where I was treated. I must have been in shock because the pain was not that bad, as I rode in the EMS to the hospital I looked at my arms as they swelled and the pain intensified. The EMS tech a women said "what you trying to be the HULK", I laughed, it was cool to take my mind off my pain. There was a throbbing and my skin was puffy, the pain became greater and greater. When we got to the hospital I walked in and sat in the ER. Like before all the nurses came around and said "it must be a fire." I made the whole floor smell like fire. The doctors all asked each other do you smell fire. The nurses flirted with me as they got to work on me right away. I enjoyed the treatment that I was given, it made me feel important. They cleaned off my arms with sterile water, and explained that they didn't want to touch the boils that were forming on my arms. They told me that inside the blister boils contained chemicals that will help my arms heal. The body creates it's own medicine, and nothing works better than that. He showed me this cream they have that is made with pure silver called silverdene, and this is the best manmade medicine. For my arms to heal it is better not to let the boils burst. "You have a third degree burn this is the worst burn that you can get" said the doctor. "round your face, neck and ears are all second degree burns. For the next days coming up the burn will get worst when it reaches the last damage stage then it will start to heal." "I'll write you a prescription for the pain, and have a nurse put some silverdene on the rest of your burns. Take care of yourself" said the doctor. "Thank You" I said as he left. Then he called a nurse to finish washing me down, and then put the silverdene on my other burns. The nurse was real nice to me she made some jokes like "what you think you're the Hulk trying to bust out of your skin" as she cleaned me and then applied the cream to my burns. When she finished with all my paperwork she gave me a canister of the silverdene cream and told me I could use their phone to call for a ride home. I called DJ a good friend to come get me, he was there real quick with his 4 X 4 Truck and gave me a ride home. They put all my fire cloths in a plastic bag to stop the smelling up the hospital. I left the hospital in their operating robe with my arms and face rapped up like the mummy. I had to stay at my parents house first until I was able to go home. My sister thanked DJ her part time boyfriend and my ace boon coon. I stayed home and milked it as long as I could, getting all the sympathy, the great war hero. Trula was worried and many other girls that I was seeing and old girlfriends also. I enjoyed my few days off. DJ would take me around if I had to go anywhere. When it was time for me to report to the Medical Department I went downtown so they could check me out. Every time we would get in an accident or injury we would have to go to the Fire department doctors to check it out. They checked me out and told me the next time I had to come there. After that the department was checking to see if I was wearing a fire coat. They felt that the burns were so severe that I must not have had my fire equipment on. What happen was that house was made with cinderblocks and only had a front window and back window, all the heat that was created from the fire stayed on the first floor just like an oven. When I stepped in the heat had to be over five hundred degrees and because their was just a few windows and a door the heat stayed in the house. The heat only dissipated after I fogged it out after putting the fire out.

Each day my arms got worst the pain grew but all this was nothing compared to my next visit to the hospital. By this time the boils were so large that you could hear the fluids splashing around inside. I had no idea what they were going to do to me next. When I arrived at Sinai Hospital for my appointment. The first few appointments all they did was rewrap my arms with cotton gauges but this time it is a drastic change. The nurse first took off all the bandages and the doctor came in with these scrapers and began to scrub my arms. The pain I felt was excruciating, the pain from the burn alone was bad but this was like no pain I ever felt. Women say men don't know pain, but with this doctor scrapping all the old skin off my arm it was hell. The smell was ghastly. It looked like the Grand Canyon, the valley was all the burned skin they scrapped off. I could see the different layers of skin as they were stripped off. This time I could of screamed louder than ever, getting burned was nothing compared to this. That's why I thought it wasn't that bad because the heat burned my nerves. Now that they are working it's time to scrape the old skin off. This is the reason I didn't want to be a doctor because this kind of work I couldn't do. The best thing about it was they did try to go fast, but it was hard for me to hold still. Water boarding, nails under the fingernail, a knife cutting off fingers, in my mind there was nothing more painful than scrapping newly formed nerve endings with whatever it was they were using. It looked like just a sponge but it felt like sandpaper, or a Brillo pad. I don't know how I made it through that but if I had any secrets I would of told them with pleasure. I was sweating, tears were forming, my body was shaking like a leaf, the pain was unbearable. It took me a while to get myself together so I could leave. After scraping all the boils and dead skin off I could see all the layers that were destroyed by the heat. It looked like the pictures of skin in a medical book. While recuperating the department was trying to press charges against me for fighting a fire without my equipment. They did not believe that the damage was done while wearing a fire coat. Instead of giving me an honor, a badge, a certificate of valor, they wanted to reprimand me.

If my coat, helmet, gloves, air tank and mask all, were on, the temperature in that kitchen had to be the cause. Not my negligent, my bravery, my will power to stick with it. The belief that I was the best at what I do, they don't make a fire I can't put out! This is when I fell out of love with the Fire Department. I realized that I may end up dieing in a fire one day. Looking at other fire fighters showed me that if I did live I could be missing a finger, limb or scared for life. I finally started to think about myself. All the partying and whoreing I was doing was to enjoy what I could of this world before I leave. Maybe I wasn't a superhero, or in that house they had Kryptonite.

When I went back to work it wasn't long before I was transferred to Ladder 3, on Vinewood, and West Grand Boulevard. I now was looking for something meaningful in my life. The women in my life gave me pleasure but I wanted to settle down and raise a family. The life of a fireman is not a good one to raise a family on. I wanted more out of life, fighting fires, and the life I was leading didn't make it anymore. I came to a point where I was bored with this career, it could have been that this engine house had very little fires. I partied all the time and was heavy drinking, going to the Detroit West Club, on Thursdays, The Warehouse downtown Fridays and Saturdays, Wednesdays Floods, or The Sting, there was a party every night and the Long Islands were flowing. I would meet someone out new or ladies that I already had a relationship with. I was totally honest with them I felt I was a Player and I was proud of it. The problem was no matter who I was with there was always someone else. I did enjoy the relationships I had but it was always another conquest, a new young lady that I was after.

Through it all Trula stuck with me for what ever reason she did. I was impressed by her will power. She didn't complain and through the summers I was so busy I would usually see her again in the fall when I slowed down. When I was with her I was bored when we were apart I wanted her. "Break-up to Make-up, that's all we do. First you love me, then you hate me, it's a game for fools." She was my True Love I always confessed, but there was something about me that I couldn't settle down. I was now twenty four and I had everything I wanted: a house, three cars, a Van, a drop top Convertible Lemans, a Mercedes Benz, and all the women I wanted. There were so many women I couldn't get to some because there wasn't enough time in a day, and I was always looking for a new one. Then something happened that changed everything. Trula got pregnant and she wanted to keep her. I got women pregnant before but I always paid for an abortion, and I paid for many, some real and some fake it didn't matter to me. In fact when she became pregnant three others girls did at the same time. She was the first that said she wanted to keep the baby. I guess all the other girls knew I was out for just fun, so they had abortions. Some got pregnant that didn't tell me and they got rid of the baby without saying anything to me. I guess when you don't believe in God it doesn't make a difference.

Just to think that she wanted to be with me let me know no matter how bad I was made me think better of her. I never thought for a second that this was done on purpose, and if it was I was still flattered. I think we messed up our relationship because when I tried to talk to her she turned me down. We were friends and I loved her because I knew she was there for me, and I thought that I would never be able to find someone that would love me more. All she put up with, we started on the wrong foot, and she should of put her foot down long ago instead of letting me get away with everything. In fact it was because she was so easy that I did what I did to her.

I asked her to marry me, it was the right thing to do. I guess it was the way I was raised. The problem was the closer it got to the date the colder my feet got. I was very unhappy with my life, I wanted to be more than a fireman. I wanted to be an actor, and I felt the longer I go on with this fire department one day I was going to be killed at work. My face with cuts and stitches, my arms carried the marks from that third degree burn, all other burns where healed except for on my back. I wanted to be a actor but I felt like Frankenstein the monster. The wedding day got closer and I tried to call it off, but I was told by my mother that it was too late. On the wedding day I got lost and didn't show up, and the wedding was at my father's house and she was 6 months pregnant and showing. It was hell, there were death threads and fights, but I was on my way out of town.

Chapter 9
THE RUNAWAY

HOLLYWOOD HERE I COME, WITH my writer friend O, I set out for fame and my name in lights. I resigned from the fire department and flew to Los Angeles. I got there and lived with my brother Con he was a going to school for music at Valley College in L.A. It was like a reunion all my brothers were there. When I got to LA the first thing I did was go to the beach and run out to the biggest wave and body surf the day away. I was having so much fun and I got turned around in the waves that I started swimming out to sea. I was swimming for about a hour and I got tired so I started to go back to the shore. I swam about another thirty minutes the wrong way. This was the first time swimming in a long time and I was dead tired. I stopped moving and just floated down all the time thinking about Trula. She just got finished talking to me about swimming. She was a Olympic swimmer, she told me to relax and be one with the water, don't fight it. This time I swam to the top and looked for the shore, then I took my time and slowly swam toward it. The waves kept pushing me farther and farther out, but I kept on swimming. It was like I was running. She told me at the right pace I could swim forever, and I believed her. By this time I got closer and closer and the lifeguards saw me, but it was too late because I was already at the shore. A lifeguard gave me a float and a crowd came up with my brothers. I walked out of the sea wore out, dead tired. This little incident foretold my whole trip. Rod and Con came running to see if I was okay. They laughed and we had a good time. In my mind I knew if it wasn't for Trula, I would be drown.

I went out and applied for the LA Fire Department, the Sheriff Deputy, and the Beverly Hill police department. While I was in LA, I had the time of my life and in the best shape ever, running 5 to 10 miles a day working out everyday, swimming two to three miles one day, 100 push-ups, 200 sit-ups looking the best in my life. D and I would comb the beaches for beautiful women, this was my escape and I had the time of my life.

We had a good time getting to know each other again, playing chess all night. I got a job working at Bob's Big Boys as a cook. I tried looking for a job acting and modeling, but I didn't like the cattle calls. I learned a lot about Hollywood and the business of Entertainment. I did have a good time at the beach and meeting some beautiful women. I was in the best shape of my life, then I ran into Brenda Starr. She had a boyfriend and she set me up with her girlfriend, Helena. The real reason I was here was I heard Brenda was here, the Love of my life. I always dreamed that we would get back together one day. Helena was real nice a short light brown lady with short curly hair, her mother owned a resale shop by our apartment. She was real nice, a valley girl. One night after we made love we heard Brenda and her boyfriend making love and it sounded like they had a lot more fun than we did. They were making these noises that just turned us on. Helena and I would sit at the bottom of the stairs together and listen to them carrying on night after night. Helena was one of those girls that would tell you exactly what to do while having sex and it wasn't fun. I couldn't complain because something is better than nothing. I wanted more and she wasn't giving it to me, she was kind of fragile. One day when Brenda's boyfriend was gone I crept up to her room and got in her bed naked. She put me out. I could have been wrong about her, I guess she grew up. Yes I was still in love with her, I thought. Can I blame all my problems on her I guess not she always told me she just liked my body. Her boyfriend was younger finer and half white, like her. I must have been crazy to even try it. I had to try. I learned if it was something you wanted go for it. I did mess up with her girlfriend. She looked good and was real nice. Yes Brenda told on me and it was a real mess, can I say that she turned me into the man I was.

They came to my brothers house to confront me. Her boyfriend said he could understand, I thought we were one big happy hippy commune, I guess not. I remember when I dreamed that I married her and we moved to Los Angeles, she was my Endless Love, my first love. I ran for love for so long. I was such a romantic that it takes a long time for an ex-love to dissipate. Maybe I had to get her out of my head before I got married.

After taking the three hour test for the Los Angeles Fire Department and failing it because of vocabulary really put a stop to my plans. Then I pass the Deputy Sheriff's test. We were working with my brother selling cable television. It was fun and I won some awards for selling On-TV. This was my first sales job, we went door to door. I worked with my brother who got the job for me. They had sales meeting and prizes for the most sold. The company had and baseball team we would play with them. I enjoyed all my brothers friends. One day they had a picnic and it was close to a theme park. Ray my brother D and I caught the bus late when we got there it was over. To get back to the bus stop on time we had to go though Magic mountain. We decided to sneak into Magic mountain, it was so close it seemed like a good idea. We all make it but Ray got caught then he fingered me. That sure ended my plans to join any police department. Everything I tried to do even acting in movies or dancing on television nothing would work. Our writer O had leave because his son got very sick. Without him we couldn't get into the film industry because he was the writer of the group.

Well none of my plans worked out, my writer friend came back home first, I paid his way his son was sick. My brother laughed at me when I said I was going back to my job and to get married to Trula. My younger brother D said just answer me one question "when one of those old girl friend run into you what are you going to do". I said "I will do my best to not mess with any of them", I was going to settle down and be a good husband. I came back, got married and got my job back. She was going to school at WCCC and I was working again at the Fire Department.

My brother warned me that if I went back to get married I'd go back to my old habits. I didn't let that slow me down, I believed that it would work for Trula and I. She was a model that wanted to work on rehabbing homes together. I was a fire fighter that wanted to become a star, I came back with my hopes crushed. It didn't matter because what I came back to was the best I could ever hoped for. A beautiful girl and a wonderful baby, my daughter was born while I was in LA. We got married as soon as I got back, and I went to work for the Fire Department again. I loved being married, but I soon found out that my wife wanted something else. She wasn't happy with how I kept her shut out. My "Player rules" were hard to give up. The best way she got me was to do everything I wanted. We made Love like we were meant to be together, there was no one better than her, and she was always ready. To tell the truth I couldn't keep up with her, she always wanted it.

What I did know was that the true answer to how will I know what Love is. Son you can love anyone if you try hard enough, you need to be careful of who you love. Before you make a choice understand why you are making that decision and be very careful. The question that needs to be answered is why do you want to love this person. What are her goals, do they match with yours, that means will they work together. I was so ready to go out and look for love, yet I didn't know what I was looking for. The world is so large that we decide to experience it rather than formulate what would be best for our lives. What was even worst I wanted only what looked beautiful first, personality was second, long terms goals didn't matter to me. Although we did exchange what we wanted to do in life when I would meet a new lady. From the very beginning of a relationship most times we would talk about our life dreams, hopes, and careers. I didn't know, that I was being programmed with every relationship. Whatever was good in that one I wanted in the next, and the bad I wanted to stay away from. I fought against marriage so hard I was so scared of it, I ran all the way to LA, and when nothing would work out I had to come back to it.

When you make a bad decision in your life there are signs showing you where you are headed. Everything I did wanted, the closeness, the honesty, becoming one person, then I changed, and the game did also. Some of the same old excuses I used to give were given to me, and I thought I was the first to say that. I remember when I would start a fight or an argument just so I could go out. Now it's being done to me. The main lesson I learned was that what goes around comes around. After fighting marriage for so long I grew to love it, someone else taking care of me, and doing the same. Going to bed with the same person everyday can create a special bond between two people. I always knew that marring Trula was the right thing to do, just at the wrong time. I wanted to marry her. I needed to know what was my life purpose was and, the career that went along with it. Without this I could not find True Love, because I would always be looking for my purpose in the world. Yes a beautiful women could complete the package but she can't become my whole life. Unless she leads me to my total purpose and lets me discover it for myself. To complete any good and lasting marriage both parties have to work hard at building up each other, and guiding each to the best future.

While in this mode of relationships my desires were changed by someone that loved me. It was the care and attention that she gave me changed my mind. If Trula was to sell marriage like Cassandra it might have worked better. The problem was that she didn't know what she wanted either, so she couldn't sell the package. In fact after she got pregnant I asked her to marry me but the problem was that we had an open relationship, and she didn't know how to close it. She could have said that I let you get away with all your messing around because of the way I took you from Cassandra. She could have laid down her rules of marriage, even though I already knew we still should have talked about it. If she was my first girlfriend I think it work have worked better. At eighteen if Trula was my first girlfriend a lot would be different. She might not have even been attracted to me, if I wasn't a fireman. Her first career choice was a model in which she was very good at. It was a boyfriend that was a photographer that talked her into being a model. This was the same boyfriend she left for me. Her mother told her there was more of a future with me because of my job. That might be the reason she ended her relationship, when I said I was going to marry some else. She knew I was a nice guy and her mother could be right.

To tell the truth bad relationships can help by teaching what should be done in the new ones, with the proper prospective. There will always be bad relationships and there is no way of avoiding them. It would be nice for the first relationship be the only one but we don't live in fairy tales. Experience is the best teacher, trying to protect myself from harm seems impossible. In the end all that I let in my heart hurt me, so I now know that there is no way to protect yourself from this pain. If you love, you will be hurt one day.

Chapter 10

A FAMILY MAN

IT TOOK ME A FEW months before I was back to work.
They stationed me at Engine 21 on Linwood. It wasn't
bad, a pretty fast engine house. Some old friends and
some new ones it was a good engine house. On the Corner
was a fish Carry-out and working inside was Yah Yah my
old roommate. He gave me the lowdown on all the girls
in the neighborhood. We had many fires there in mostly
two family flats because the area was full of them. This
used to be a Jewish area and they built two family flats so
their families could stay together. I always took cot watch
because after Engine 49 I loved it. It was cool everybody
else will go to sleep and the city would come alive at
night. Nightlife in Detroit is like nothing anywhere else,
the Parties the Clubs, the people out to party. I would sit
right in front of the station at night all lights off. It was
always a show something going on, ladies on their way out

would stop and talk. Late night my girl came from my old hood, Lois Martin she just became a fire fighter right before my brothers class. Lois was Glen's sister he was a good friend of mine from Griggs street. Back in the day I was walking on the Park down from the school and these three boys jumped me. I knew a lot of people from my brothers and my paper route. Glen's little gang jumped me they were just playing. I at the time was leader of the pack so this didn't bother me. I was about six feet they were five feet and smaller than I, because Glen was a few years younger than I. I did pretty good for three to one and showed them some moves they didn't know. Glen and I stayed friends for years, but his sister Lois I barely knew. All I knew was that she was super fine, Miss. Brick House, Brown skinned with freckles and Spanish features, she would always have two or three fine girlfriends with her. She came in the Engine house after a party with two of her girlfriends. They all were fine and dressed up, Lois worked on the other unit and she would come see me some times. Her fine ladies with her would come and flirt with me. We went to a few concerts together I loved her as a sister.

After that we got a run by Calvert street a fire in a two family flat. The biggest problem with this area is more people to get out of the house. Two parents, more children, grandparents, uncles and aunts. We have to be very careful to make sure all are saved. When we pulled up I put on my tank and grab an axe. Search and rescue are the Truck mission, while waiting for water. We got almost everyone out in time. I went to look for a man in the basement. I found him in a corner confused. I walked him out, right after we got water. When the water dripped to the basement it was so hot it burned my neck. We walked through the hot water to get out of the basement and his daughter was glad to see him. They walk up to him a hugged him and put a sheet around him. She looked me in the eye and said thank you. We had many fires up and down Linwood but none touched me more.

Getting used to being married and not free to go to the bars and hang. This was my way of hanging, to sit on the outside of the station watching. The club life I used to live was like a drug calling an addict. I tried to be the best father and husband going to church and out with my family. My wife said my mind wasn't there, I wasn't letting her in, and I guess it was true. It took me a long time to build up armor against a beautiful women so I could control myself. I have not ever became so strong as to stop a beautiful woman from controlling me. Saying no to women has been hard for me, saying no to anyone is a problem. I had everything I wanted but still I wanted something else. My soul was wanting. I thought it was the pleasure of a beautiful women, but it was not. When I used to go to parties I always went after the finest lady in the room. I would settle for whoever I ended up with, but settling became my new problem, because I got the finest wife possible.

We had this fire that represented my life and how I felt at the time. When we pulled up everyone was setting up, some went in through the front and others took the back door. I saw these legs hanging out the window. I went to help whoever that was, when I got there I tried to pull him out but he wouldn't budge. I pulled and I pulled but I got no where. I didn't want to leave him but from where I was I couldn't help him either. I was scared to pull too hard because I kept on feeling like his legs were going to come off in my hands. I was so confused I didn't know what to do. Finally some one from the inside came and helped me. The plaster from the ceiling fell on his head and he was stuck right there in the window. He was knocked cold but when we got him out he was alive. This was my life, my wife was swell she did everything that she thought I wanted. At this time I lived on Birchcrest with my parents. It was beautiful having a new born baby but it was scary too she was so fragile the first baby for me was all pins and needles. I wanted to do everything right, I took a natural child birth class before I went out of town, and Trula taught me everything else I needed to know. She bought a book on child birth and we red it together. We would read to the baby through her stomach. Those days were all so happy for me I ran away from what I wanted most. The reason I went to Hollywood, I was scared of being injured for life, not being sure I was ready to settle down, and wanting a career that was more fulfilling. When Trula got out of college she went to work for the city in the forest department. She use to work in parks and recreation as a lifeguard. I helped out when she was at work with the baby, my mother helped also.

Jesse Bigham a son of my father's best friend lived around the corner, and visited often. He was always trying to come up with a plan to become a millionaire. He was currently working with a lawn care company that he started. He had business cards and many customers in the area, and he was doing well. All I would do is take care of the baby when Trula was at work. When she got home I would go over Jesse's house and visit him. One day he was thinking if he could get one dollar from everyone he knew how much money would he have. He talked me into getting a beeper because he said as a fireman I could to be contacted anywhere I went. This technology was cool and I liked it that way Trula could call me anytime she needed me. We came up with many schemes to make money and none of them really worked. My father said that there are no get rich quick schemes and that you have to work long and hard to establish any good business. I only had one problem boredom, like it was said idle time is the Devils playshop. I was happy, Trula had everything I wanted and she was so sweet, I just became bored with her. Something was missing I was happy but, why do I always fall in love with women I can't have and grow bored with women that want me.

Just like my brother said before I left Hollywood, that I had too many women in Detroit, and sooner or later I was going to get caught up. Before I fell for one of the many women I knew in Detroit. Many tried I ran into many that tempted me. It seemed as if there was a special attraction to me because I was married. All kinds of beautiful women tried to get me to mess with them, to just touch them, and it was getting so hard to resist. My wife was so good to me she did nothing wrong, anything I asked for she did, you couldn't get a better wife.

It wasn't just the women at the clubs, there were so many beautiful ladies at work on Linwood. Just my luck, Yah-Yah worked next door at the fish market. It was more women walking the streets pasting the station. Resisting to the temptations that went back and forth all day long. Sitting in front of the station was just an invitation. This was a area that I never came to, but I was surprised at all the good looking women. Good thing this was a busy fire house.

I was then transferred to Engine 8 on Lafayette and Tenth. This was a slow engine house close to downtown across from the main post office. One good boss, one bad boss, it was an okay station, we could go days without a fire. What I really hated was the details to a southwest Detroit all white prejudice station on Junction and Rogers. It was so bad that I would sit in my van all day, we didn't get along so I just stopped talking to them. I refused to eat with them and they got mad at me and got the chief to order me to. The chief told me that if I didn't cooperate that he would send me to the far eastside if I lived on the westside. He told me that he would take care of me, and not in a nice way. I told my mother and she told my father, he called the commissioner Melvin Jefferson who was a good friend of his. They were both appointees under the Young administration. The next day I was called downtown to have a meeting with the Chief of the Department Masters. He sat me down and apologized for the other Chief cussing me out, and he said that he was an asshole. Then he told me that I was a good fire fighter and they never had any problem out of me. That I shouldn't pay any attention to that Chief, he's a trouble maker. I never had another problem with that officer but I still didn't like working on that truck. One day they thought I left because they didn't see me all day, I was in my van and just came in to jump on the truck for a fire run. I tried to stay to myself and just watch television or in the front till night. We just didn't get along so I didn't want to eat with them, I felt that I had that option. When I would cook if someone didn't want to be in it was no big deal. From a certain point of view it did look like I was the trouble maker. A real cook could of made other things that didn't cost so much or they could of put up more money each and have what they wanted.

When I was detailed to Engine 1 and Engine 9 things were real nice. Both were downtown Detroit the Nightlife and crowds were very enjoyable. I was asked to cook many times because of my reputation as a good cook. When I was at Engine 1 all the big Chiefs worked there and I was known as one of their favorite cooks, I cooked there many times. There were white chiefs and black ones also. Sergeant Ned from Engine 53 was now the Lieutenant at Engine one. He was a different boss then what he used to be he was now by the book. Most officers that made it up to higher ranks changed. The Chief of Department Watkins was a whole different person. I remember Watkins when I first went to engine 42. He had a fleet of ice cream trucks, he was a real nice and fun person. Maybe it was the weight of the department on his shoulders. The fire department we were on has a seniority system, the ones with the most time had the best positions. The Fire Department was like many departments of the city of Detroit where they could only do so much. It was like a political system, if there was a problem or someone made a mistake the Chief would take the blame. Then they would fire him and put the next in line in his position. I called it the scapegoat system instead of fixing the problem just put the blame on the Chief and fire him. The next chief would inherit the same system with all the same problems. They didn't have enough money to hire more workers or to get better equipment so there would be injuries and accidents because of out-dated fire engines.

In the thirteen years that I fought blazes I thought I had super powers. I felt that I could do anything. Although in the back of my mind I knew that one day I would have my last fire. Live by the sword, die by the sword, or maybe it was just time to pay for my sins. I was at the slowest engine company ever. Sometimes we wouldn't have a good fire for weeks. We just came and sat around all day with nothing to do but eat, read, watch television, and ride around downtown in the fire engine. This was a station they would put you where no one else wanted, and because I had no seniority by leaving the fire department and coming back. I had no choice, take this or nothing. Engine 21 was a good station, fires, action, women. This station was dead, no traffic, no nightlife, just factories. Many didn't like my ability to get back on the fire department so quickly. When I went to the Commissioner to resign he told me if I come back with in one year. He will hire me back. When I made my mind up to come back. I called my mother, she called my father, he called the commissioner. My father and the Commissioner were good friends I got back on but at the worst stations. You would think a slow station would be fun but I missed fighting fires. It would be at the slowest station in the city that I fought my last fire.

This brings me to my last fire. It was at Engine 8, we were having problems with our Pumper. When we were called to a fire it wouldn't pump water, the shop was called and they tried to fix it many times. Every time we pulled up to a fire we knew that we would not get any water out of this engine. The problem could be that it was too old and can't be fixed. Well the last unit told a good friend of mine who was the engineer for the day that we had a problem pumping water. He checked the engine out and got it to pump water in the morning. By the middle of the day we had a fire going throughout, from top to the bottom it was blazing. It was a four bedroom colonial and it was raging, flames coming out all the windows. Another engine pulled up and dumped it's tank into the fire. He knocked some of the fire down. When we got there I jumped off in front of the house with both bundles. I took one of the pipes to the back of the house, and another fire fighter took the other to the front. Just like before on the last few days when he tried to start pumping nothing came out. I knew there was a problem with the engine. I was ready because the engineer said he was going to get water. I knew him, he was a man that you could believe in. We waited, I had my line under my arm and stood in position to attack the fire. The engineer revved the engine higher, and higher, but still no water. These engines have enough power to send water up a hundred floors in the Renaissance Building. This engineer was determined to get water so he revved the engine even higher. All of a sudden with a burst of power the water broke through. BAM! The pressure was so high that in the front of the house the line broke loose and broke a fire fighter's leg. In the back where I was as the line filled I opened it, and whoosh the power of the pressure in the line took me in the air. I flew around wrestling the line like a live giant snake. It whipped me back and forth around a crowd of fire fighters about five or six watching. If I had of let go of this line it could of taken out many fire fighters. I held on for dear life, and shut off the line as it slammed me down on a slab of concrete 17 feet away. I had the air tank on my back and I hit the ground so hard I was knocked unconscious. I woke up with a about six fire fighters standing around me. They asked me if I could get up. When I tried I couldn't move. They grabbed me by my coat and legs carrying me to the squad. They rushed me to the hospital where I did gain my movement later, so scared I pulled myself together and crept up and out of there as fast as I could. I don't know why I was so afraid of Hospitals and I had to get out as quick as possible. They put me off for a couple of days and then sent me back to work. I saw FF Osborn and he told me that he saw me flying in the air like Superman. I was finally airborne what I always wanted to be, a flyer. When I went back to work I was riding the tiller bucket and the bumping started to hurt my back. I noticed that as the days when on my back was giving me more and more problems and pain. I couldn't get to sleep at night. I went off duty again this time, never to come back.

I was sent to the Medical Department and they sent me to many doctors, each said that there was no problem with my back, and that the problem was all in my head.

My mother hired a lawyer and we took the city to court. I was taken off the books and was off work for more than a year. This hurt me mentally after all that I had given to the fire department, my youth and now for them to act like nothing was wrong with me. I went about the whole thing wrong but I didn't know, all this was new to me. I was supposed to stay in the hospital longer for them to feel that this was a serious injury. The way they found out if an injury was real was by neglecting you for a year and if it wasn't real you would come back to work. It seemed like the whole fire department turned their back on me. After all these years now I have nothing to show for my dedication to the force. All this happened when I needed to be working. I had a business on the side and without my income I would lose everything. I just did nothing for a whole year waiting to see what the fire Department was going to do.

Many times after receiving serious injuries the Detroit fire department accused me of doing something wrong. First it was my coat and gloves, like a fire fighter would fight a fire without them. Where is the problem? Make better equipment always work on newer and better inventions for the future. Who is buying the equipment and how do they determine what to get? I heard from an accountant on the fire department and how they bought and sold fire equipment. He told me their will always be misappropriation of funds with our political system.

Fire trucks were bought and sold to made money and not just for the use of fighting fires. Some trucks we never used but we needed them while they gave us broken down trucks that ended up hurting firemen. Who is really to blame for my accident or was it a set-up to kill me.

I was sent to many doctors again this time by my Lawyer. I took a MRI which produced evidence that I had a herniated disk in three different places. The fire department turned their backs on me, and I was very hurt not just physically but emotionally. I never thought this would happen to me, but I do understand. To keep on fighting fires they must believe that nothing can hurt them. This will help them to do their jobs they must fill, invincible this will give them more power. The power of the mind is very strong in the Bible at the tower of Babel God said that" when they worked with one accord it is nothing that they can't do." When God created the world he first said " let there be light" and then their was light. Declaring what is to be done with words first is an empowering action. By fire fighters speaking to the fire, we can do many wondrous deeds. This will empower us to do these great works. For I spoke my own demise, I knew one day I would have a fire that I wouldn't come back from "Thank God" that I am still alive!

When I went to the back specialist he told me he could do a two operations for the price of one. That was a joke and it wasn't funny to me at the time. My Doctor told me that they could do the operations but they may not work. They could do the operation and I might not be able to walk again. He said that it may heal on its own with time, but if I get hurt again like that one I might not be able to stand up straight. The back is very complex and we don't know much about it we are still experimenting and learning more all the time. He said that it wasn't just that accident. The many others I had all add up, falling down the stairs in fires, and at the fire scene.

My father had Quadruple bypass surgery a while back. He changed from smoking and drinking and he is looking good. Back when he was working under Watts who was in charge of DPW for the city, in the winter whenever it snowed he would have to get up and go in to work. He was in control of the salt trucks and all the streets in the city. My father was very dedicated to his job and I think he loved it, and I was proud of him. When he took over the DPW Department the media tried to fry him on how much he made as an appointee. He had a battle with a local Detroit artist who would create art out of vacant buildings. Now some thought this was art but my father thought it was junk so he tore the houses down. There were so many vacant houses in the city they created many problems. Fires were just one of the many problems including drug houses, children being raped and no tax money. There wasn't enough money in the budget to destroy them all so he would destroy the one that posed the most problems. In the midst of this my father had an heart attack and drove himself to the hospital. We all thought my father was going to die. My brother and I were working for the fire department then. The abilities of Doctors today is extraordinary and my father came out well.

I guess everyone has their own opinion but I do remember while working at Engine 21 I had a swelling in my neck. I was diagnosed with a tumor in my throat. I had a good doctor who lived across the street from us,

Dr. Phillips, he got sick and someone just took over his practice. I was told I had a tumor by this new doctor. After my operation he found out he was wrong and I just had a stone in my gland. This was after he ripped out one of my saliva glands. I tried to sue but because I wouldn't pay the bill, I couldn't sue. Now if this is going to be anything like that I'm out! It was hard to think of getting an operation. I didn't trust them, but I will trust God. If he wants my back to be healed he will do it.

After more than a year in limbo I won my case. I had many people tell me that nothing was wrong with me. I guess everyone formed their own opinion. If they had seen the accident there would have been no problem. I also should have stayed off my feet longer, I just don't like being in hospitals. I got out of there as soon as possible which didn't help my case. An accident like that I should of stayed in for two or three days but I was out that evening. When I was able to stand and walk again I got my cloths and went home that night.

The way I lived my life when I wasn't sure if there was a God, is the way many people are living today. Things that people do when they feel there is no God, and no one is watching them. Even when I felt there was no God, I tried to be right. Some things that my friends did I could never do, because of the way I was raised. No matter if God was real or not I still believed many of the teaching I was taught. One person told me that this God stuff was made up so we would try to be good. The truth is if there was no God there would be no world, or people. That is why without God this world would be a real hell. It seems that many people want to do right or good in this world. The way I was raised was to help the needy and poor if I could, not only help my brother but a stranger if possible. I do have the drive to get to the top, but not by stepping on my brothers. I feel that my friends need to be there so we could enjoy our lives, as a community. I always enjoyed helping others and this was my true calling. To be young was beautiful doing just as you feel like is fun, why not enjoy yourself? Then to get older with all you have learned from life and this world, choices are made with care and study. In my youth I sought the fun or pleasure for the day. Then the next day what more, I had very few long range plans. After my goals were taken from me, my dreams denied, I went further and found my plan were already made.

My one true question to God was why should I follow you and do as you say? You don't know what I want, I don't even know what I want. In my teen years I felt that I could do anything I wanted to. When I reached adulthood I was told there are things that negro's are limited in doing. By my nineteenth birthday many laws and practices were being changed not just in Detroit but all over the world. (The movement that was started in India moved here in America flowed over to Africa. Nonviolent as a movement in the Bible started with Jesus moved to conquer the world) The sixties was a very successful time in Detroit,

The Car Companies were the Masters, and a small music label

Motown filled the air with music around the world with Hit after hit thus the name "Hitsville". Many things changed in the seventies the first black mayor Coleman A. Young ran Detroit for the next decade. Just as I was told what a Black man could do the rules changed again. The Detroit Fire Department became fifty percent black and has stayed that way even in the new millennium. The eighties was hard for the city with lay-offs and cut-back many people left to follow the jobs. This made a rise in fires because of two problems vacant homes and buildings, and lost revenue. City workers were forces to live in the city this made it harder on whites who wanted to live farther out in the suburbs. When this rule was changed many more left the city, a city of 2 million has slowly become 1 million and then even smaller. By the time the Nineties came a new mayor was elected the youngest mayor ever elected. The problems Detroit had were always there, but who will really solve them must be real thinkers and not politicians. Not just thinkers but doers also, men and women of action with concrete plans that won't take no for an answer. Now our whole economy is about to turn over and the stable Banks and Car Czars are no more.

America is changing now the Government is taking on many private businesses, or giving them millions to stay a flout. In all my businesses they have never offered me money to keep going, when I did have a grant to do a movie they didn't finish paying the money to complete to project. First the Banks now the Car companies, then the Radio and Television stations, our government is putting their hands in so many different private businesses. We are suppose to be a capitalistic society not a monarchy president Bush and his control has put us into a backspin while the wealthy leaders are doing everything to create more riches for themselves. If anything we need to be doing is creating peace worldwide, and not starting conflicts. There is enough wealth for everyone on earth if the greed was eliminated. There is enough land to grow food so no one will go hungry. There are enough jobs where everyone could be happily employed. I will always push for a better future for our world. Detroit is still ready, the power here can never be denied, while businesses are fighting to stay alive, the new Entertainment Capital will begin here.

A PSALM OF DAVID

Psalms 37: 1—9

" Fret not yourself because of the wicked, be not envious of wrongdoers!

For they will soon fade like the grass, and wither like the green herb.

Trust in the Lord, and do good; so you will dwell in the Land, and enjoy security.

Take delight in the Lord, and he will give you the desires of your heart.

Commit your way to the Lord; trust in him, and he will act.

He will bring forth your vindication as the light, and your right as the noonday.

Be still before the Lord, and wait patiently for him;

Fret not yourself over him who prospers in his way,

Over the man who carries out evil.

For the wicked shall be cut off;

But those who wait for the Lord shall possess the Land."

Fireman's favorite Recipes

Some of my fireman meal Plans

All of my recipes I learned from first my mother then her sister Aunt Jewell, my father was a good cook also. Most of my recipes are from firemen but they have the twist of my mothers and sister's Cajun background, and Bob's Big Boy in Los Angeles.

I always belief in the use of fresh vegetables and spices. My Mother Nora was one of the best bakers of Rolls, Cakes, Pies I hope her gift fell to me.

My Favorite Fire House Meals

There are meat markets in every town get to know the butcher, ask questions and be friendly with them. Remember they will be supplying your families food, that is very important. What made firemen food so good for you is that everything was fresh. We would buy the food the same day we prepared it. All the best firemen cooks knew some meat market where they could get the best deals on good fresh meat. My friend is Patrick at Kaps Meat in Eastern Market, he gives me the best deals around. You have to find your own but if your around tell Pat I said hello.

How I estimate the amount to make is by counting the serving for each person. For small engine houses 4 men, double houses 8—12 men, full house 12—30 men. For each meal I would have a half pound of meat per each person, and one cup vegetable, or dessert per each person.

All meals were served with a tossed salad, fresh tomatoes, cucumbers, radishes, bell peppers, lettuce, cabbage, spinach, fresh bread, many selections rye, French, onion roll, pumpernickel, cornbread, rolls, wheat, and white.

The best meal made with ground beef is freshly ground hamburger from round steak or chuck steak. My mother and firemen used a meat grinder to make not just hamburger but sausages too!

Meatloaf and gravy
Start with the meat, small house 2 pounds, large house 4 pounds of ground chuck beef,
Mix in a large bowl with a diced onions, garlic, and green pepper, half cup each small house, large house full cup, season with sea salt, Italian seasonings, two eggs small, four large, make into large loafs, put in a drain roasted in the oven set at 350, cook for an hour drain off extra oil,

put tomato paste or ketchup over the top a cook another 30 to 45 minutes, the meat should brown pull out when an even brown color in on the meat, do not over cook it will dry out, let cool before slicing.

mashed potatoes
Peel potatoes cut into cubes boil until a fork can glide through easy, then drain, mix with butter sea salt or seasoned salt, can milk or regular milk, mash with a potato masher until smooth with no lumps, serve with chopped chives or parsley mix in.

green bean casserole
Green beans mixed with cream of mushroom soup in a casserole dish, do not add water, one cup of milk mix with soup, put fired onion on the top, put in over set at 350 for one hour, or until top browns.

Stuff Pork chops
Start with two inch thick pork chops, clean meat with cold water, then season it with power garlic, onion, sea salt or season salt, poultry season, paprika, then flour both sides, cut a pocket in the middle of the chop, insert stuffing and place on the cookie sheet, put in over set at 350 degree for an hour check, cook another thirty minutes, when meat turns brown it's done, do not over cook that will dry out the meat. When using thinner cuts of meat you can cut down the cooking time.

Fried pork chops season the same, then flour, and fry on medium high till light brown on both sides, then put on a drainable roaster pan and put in oven at 350 degrees for 30 minutes.

Steak

The choice of meat is very important Porterhouse is the best cut then T-bone, then New York, look for a marbling red with white in the texture of the meat, this will be juicier, clean meat with cold water, heat a cast iron skillet on high, or on a grill, cook until it browns then turn it over, pull off in a few minutes its rare, wait a little longer, it's medium, longer medium well, longer well done. Fry Onions, mushrooms, bell pepper, in the pan afterwards a little water and brown sugar, until they brown add a little corn starch or flour to stiffen the sauce. Serve the steaks over the sauce or without and use sauce as a side.

Fire house Spaghetti

Cook meat, Ground Round or Ground Chuck, Italian Sausage, Pork Sausage, cook and drain oil, mix onions, garlic, thyme, rosemary, in beef sauté set aside, cook separately tomato sauce, and boil water with salt and one drop of oil for noodles cook until they are soft then let sit for 30 minutes, rinse with cold water, start cooking tomatoes sauce, mix in tomato paste, stewed tomatoes, basil, thyme, parsley, oregano, onions, garlic, three tablespoons of brown sugar slowing cook on low fire for one hour, then mix in meats after breaking them down into small pieces or meat balls slice Italian sausages then cook slowly for thirty minutes, add bell pepper last, meal can be served mixed with noodles, or on top of noodles.

Lasagna
Cook the same as Spaghetti but use lasagna noodles, layer meat and noodles in a oblong deep dish, first a thin layer of meat sauce, noodles lay side by side to cover completely, lay meat sauce, cover with noodles, mix ricotta cheese with two eggs, meat layer with mozzarella cheese, Colby cheese, cheddar cheese, and parmesan sprinkled on top with paprika and parsley, put in oven for one hour, when the top is golden brown pull it out and cool, don't slice until it cools.

Fire House Tacos
Cook Ground Beef pour off oil, season with garlic, onions, season salt, chili pepper, thyme, rosemary, parsley, bell pepper sauté, then tomato sauce two teaspoons of brown sugar, heat tacos in oven set at 350 for three to five minutes just to heat them, put meat in taco shells, serve with diced tomatoes, sliced lettuce, cheese, and sour cream.

Salmon croquette
Use 2 cans of salmon, mix with two eggs half onion, half, bell pepper, and one cup of cracker meal, mix in a bowl, season with sea salt, pepper, Cajun seasoning, make into

round patties, roll in corn meal, then fry on medium high brown then flip, take out put on cookie sheet and cook 20 minutes in the oven before serving.

Kielbasa and potatoes
Peel potatoes cut into slices, put in frying pan with oil, cook on medium heat, season salt and pepper cook 30 minutes add onion and garlic cook 10 minutes add kielbasa cut in slices, cook 20 minutes on low, add paprika and chives cover and serve.

Fried potatoes and onions
Cook same as Kielbasa and potatoes just don't put kielbasa in.

Fried Chicken
Clean chicken with cold water, put off any extra fat, look for feathers and hairs clean with knife or pluck, cut into pieces, season with seasoning salt, pepper, power onions, power garlic, paprika, Italian herbs, then flour on both sides, fry in a pan half filled with oil, cook skin up till light brown on both side put on flat pan in oven set at 350 for 20 minutes to catch extra grease, drain grease and serve.

Baked Chicken
Prepare like fried but put on a lightly greased rectangular pan with PAM, skin up bake in oven for an hour and a half pull out when golden brown, pour off grease mix

with corn starch or flour to make gravy season to taste add diced onions or chicken giblets.

Turkey and stuffing

Thaw turkey in refrigerator 24 hours before sitting in cold water to clean, season with season salt, poultry season, 12 hours before cooking, pull out neck, giblets cook in water bring to boil, Cook and pan of cornbread and soak old bread in milk, fry breakfast sausage, when cooked drain oil and sauté onions, bell pepper, with the sausage, in a large bowl mix the bread, corn bread, sausage with onions and bell pepper, with poultry seasoning, season salt, sliced celery, paprika, add four eggs mix well, stuff turkey and put extra in a casserole dish cook both in oven set at 350 degrees small turkey 3-4 hours larger 5 hours cook until golden brown, stuffing in casserole cook for one two hours until browns on top. After the turkey is cooked pull out stuffing right away before it cools. Always cut up the turkey in sections and separate from the dressing, store in different containers, to avoid bacteria. I started cooking turkeys without stuffing but cook the stuffing on the side. When I do I just put celery onions, bell pepper, and seasoning inside the bird when it's cooking to keep it juicy. Then I use the juice and vegetables from the turkey to make the stuffing.

Roasted Turkey wings

Clean turkey wings in cold water place in casserole dish season with season salt, pepper, garlic power, and onion power, put a little water mixed with onions, cook in oven at 350, use broiler, baste regularly with water in pan, cook for 2 hour mix in bell peppers and mix corn starch or flour with water until smooth, pour in pan and cook for one more hour

thicken up gravy, pull out let cool and serve.

Fried squash

Rinse squash with cold water, cut off end pieces and throw away, cut in slices, yellow squash, zucchini squash, onions, bell peppers sauté with corn oil or butter salt and pepper, until soft with a little browning, turn constantly evenly until done.

Cabbage

Cook the same as squash, cut in squares and fry in pan with onions, bell pepper, until soft, put a little water, season with salt and pepper, two teaspoons of sugar, cook covered with a lid, turn fire on low, serve when tender, don't cook too long.

Greens

Cook smoked turkey leg or wing in large deep pot, filled one quarter with water, season with season salt, pepper, onions, bell pepper cut very small, and two teaspoons of sugar, cook boiling for and hour, while cleaning greens, use large tub clean with cold water, rinse thoroughly, collars rinse twice, emptying tub each time, other green clean two more time emptying tub to see dirt on bottom, once clean lay leaf on top of each other and slice one inch thick cutting off large stem at bottom, put cut leafs in boiling water and cook down stirring regularly, adding more when cooks down until all is in the pot, then cover and cook taste add onion power and garlic power, to taste if bitter peel and cut a potato and put in when leaves are soft to taste they are ready.

Texas Chili

Cook beans first a day early red kidney beans, and pinto beans, cook with water ham bone, or bacon, onions seasoned with salt and pepper, keep in juices set aside, cook ground beef, ground chuck, break down into small pieces, pour out oil, season with season salt, pepper, garlic power, onion power, chili power, ground cumin, paprika, cut onions, bell pepper, garlic, and sauté with meat, then pour in tomato sauce, stewed tomatoes, three teaspoons of brown sugar, cook on low, stirring regularly, add to taste chili peppers on desired hotness, cook on low for two hours, serve in a bowl on a bed of rice.

Stuffed cabbage and Stuffed bell peppers

Chose and very lean ground beef like ground chuck, ground sirloin, mix with cooked rice drained, cook cabbage lightly till leafs are soft, don't cook bell peppers, mix chopped onions, season salt, pepper, then roll the meat mixture in the leaf, put meat mixture in a hollowed out bell pepper with top cut off, put in large deep roaster pan, fill with tomato sauce season with basil, thyme, oregano, parsley and two table spoons of brown sugar cover and put in oven set at 350, cook for an hour check cook for thirty more, turn off and sit, serve warm.

Swedish Meatballs
Start with ground chuck beef, and pork sausage or Italian sausage mix ¾ beef to ¼ sausage, mix in large bowl, add seasoning salt, pepper, rosemary, basil, thyme, oregano, diced very small onions, bell peppers, garlic, add A1 steak sauce mix and roll into balls cook in oven on 350 or fry in pan on top of stove at medium high, turn until all sides browned, pour off extra oil, mix corn starch or flour in a bowl with milk stir until smooth, spoon in sour cream, let cook at medium stirring regularly until gravy thickens up, cool and serve on top of noodles or rice.

Sweet and Sour Pork
Start with a whole end pork lion or pork shoulder, pick one with less fat more meat, clean with cold water slice into triangular pieces inch thick season with soy sauce and flour lightly fry in frying pan medium high, with a small amount of oil barely cover the pan, brown on all sides after all pieces have browned add sliced onions, bell pepper, ginger, water chestnuts, celery, carrots, pineapples, garlic sauté for 15 minutes add water just to cover then half a cup of brown sugar four tablespoons of corn starch, cook

until thicken then turn low and cook for 15 to 20 minutes covered serve over a bed of rice and bean sprouts.

Pepper Steak

Start with a round steak, sirloin, or flat steak, pick a steak that has good marbling in it, slice into long strips cut against the grain, season with soy sauce then flour lightly, fry in a large frying pan until light brown mix in onions, garlic cook together for 15 minutes then cover with water and cook on low while stirring regularly, add bell peppers, black pepper, ground ginger, three tablespoons brown sugar and cook thirty minutes stirring regularly, cook on low covered, used other peppers like yellow, red, to spice up, serve with rice or noodles.

Beef stroganoff

This is a way of cooking tougher cuts of beef, to taste as tender as a good cut of steak like a porterhouse. Select a chipped beef ,steak sirloin, or round steak, cut in short strips cut against the grain, this also adds to the tenderness of the meat the cutting is important, if your selection of meat is better quality like New York strip or prime rib you can cut them in cubes and they will keep their juice and tenderness, season with seasoning salt, power garlic, power onion, and roll in flour, prepare a large frying pan with oil just enough to cover the bottom, fry the meat on medium high, cook evenly until brown on all sides, then add onions, garlic, cook 15 minutes stirring regularly , then add water and sour cream, cover and cook on low for 30 minutes, serve with noodles.

Shrimp Fried rice
Start with a deep frying pan or wok, three or four tablespoons of oil, peel and vein shrimp sit in cold water drip dry then season with soy sauce, fry shrimp in oil with onions, garlic, celery, bell peppers, sauté add rice and brown mixing regularly, 15 minutes then add water cook on low covered till rice is cooked.

Egg Rolls
An old world treat with the new world twist, I have seen that other meats are put in an egg roll that are very good. You can buy the egg roll wrap at your grocery store. The traditional egg roll would start with cabbage, bean sprouts, onions, green onions, celery, peppers and shrimp, but the new twist is different meats like corned beef and cheese, or hamburger, steak, pork, and even crab and lobster, lay the egg roll out , put the stuffing at the bottom, fold the corners up like wrapping a Christmas present, and roll over until it's closed, then fry in a frying pan or deep fryer for 5 to 10 minutes, dry and let cool on paper towel, serve as appetizers.

Barbequed Ribs
Start with a good cut of meat, strip excess fat, peel inter line of thin fat off the rib, then wet both sides with any

type of vinegar mixture, like Italian dressing, or marinate, season with seasoning salt, pepper, garlic power, onion power, rosemary, paprika, let sit covered, for two hours, heat grill put ribs on faced down meat side up, cook until light brown then turn over cook the same, cook flipping them around to make sure all sides get cooked, after they have a nice rich brown, stack on a side with low heat, and cook slowly, baste with sauce and wrap foil around to protect from burning, turn and cook until the bone comes out of the rib at the tip, cool and serve.

Rib cooking sauce
Boil down onions, bell peppers red, green, yellow, diced with garlic, add brown sugar, stewed tomatoes, oregano, basil, thyme, parsley, cook down into thick sauce.

Barbequed short end ribs
Clean ribs with cold water, season with seasoning salt, pepper, paprika, onion power, garlic power, then cook on a grill, brown on all sides, use sauce after cooked wrap in foil let sit in low temperature, serve with baked beans.

Fruit Salad
Start with large watermelon, a bunch of bananas, grapes, cantaloupe, pineapples, melons, strawberries, blue berries, kiwi, cut or scoop melons, cut pineapple into cubes, cut kiwi into sections, mix together in large bowl, or hollowed out watermelon.

Salad
Romaine lettuce, clean with cold water drip dry cut into slices one inch thick, tomatoes sliced into quarters, leaf spinach, red cabbage sliced thin, cucumbers striped and sliced, radish diced, boiled eggs diced and sliced, mix the lettuce with the spinach and cabbage in a large salad bowl, add together serve with dressing.

Pie Dough
Put 3 cups of flour in a mixing bowl, sift in one teaspoon of salt, three tablespoons of baking power three tablespoons of sugar, mix with one cup of butter one egg and one half a cup of water and a teaspoon of vanilla extract, mix till crumby, pack together two medium balls with the dough.

Peach cobbler
Flour a cutting board large enough to fill your pie pan, use the balls of dough, roll out sprinkling flour all the time to make sure it doesn't stick, roll dough larger than the cooking dish or pie pan so it covers it completely, pinch the edge of the pie dish to form an outer crust, pour in can peaches with juice, mix with brown sugar, sugar, cinnamon, use crumbs in bowl mix with brown sugar, sugar cover the top of pie with crumb topping, put in oven set at 350 degrees for one hour and a half, until the top browns not too dark.

Apple pie

Peel and core apples, cook the peels in water with cinnamon brown sugar, drain off liquid mix with corn starch to thicken into a heavy sauce, mix in apples, pour in pie dough, cover with pie dough or crumb topping, if used pie dough make a few opening in dough before putting in oven, cook at 350 for one hour and a half, checking the color on top, cut off oven when top browns.

Fried Catfish

Soak fish in milk before seasoning, season with seasoning salt, pepper, paprika, garlic power, onion power, parsley, dip in beaten eggs then roll in mixture of flour and corn meal, fry in frying pan turn when lightly brown cook on both sides, pull out a drain off excess oil, put in oven for 20—30 minutes, serve hot.

Baked salmon

Clean salmon with cold water, season with seasoning salt, or salmon rub, paprika pepper, put on oven pan with butter and bake at 350 degrees cook skin side down for one hour, when top is lightly browned at edges take out serve with fresh lemons slices.

Soups

Soups are what the fire department lives on every morning when the new crew comes in they look through the refrigerator to see what was there. What is needed to make soup is very simple start with water boiling, add soup base onions, potatoes, celery, meat, leftovers are good, like old chicken, or a ham bone, old roast, pork shoulder, cut meat in cubes take out bones when cooked, cook on high for an hour, lower heat, season to taste with salt and pepper, garlic salt, onion power, add noodles or rice and omitt potatoes.

Pot Roast
Use English roast, chunk roast, season with seasoning salt black pepper, power garlic, onion power, then flour on both sides, fry with minimum oil, until brown on both sides then put in a deep roasting oven pan cover and cook for an hour, then add peeled and quartered potatoes onions, garlic, carrots, bell peppers, and cook for another hour with water mixed flour or corn starch, pour in for gravy.

Corned Beef
Boil Corned beef four 4 hours, pull out let dry, put in oven in a deep dish with cover, mix one cup of water with cabbage, carrots potatoes onions and bake at 350 degrees for one hour, serve with mustard and brown sugar mixture heated.

About the Author

I was always a dreamer, but to create reality from my goals proved to be quite a task. First I dealt with my physical limitations, then my mental intelligent to overcome all obstacles which lay in my path. Which include various persons instructing me of the great impossibility of my hopes and dreams. It was not until later in my life that I stop taking negative advice, because things that I've done, others could not do before me. I found out that I was blessed to find success, happiness in a career choice, and to have lived a fulfilled life

My experience with the United States Air Force changed my goals, and understanding of a career choice. I took all the tests and passed them with eighty and ninety percent scores. I was always told that I could be what ever I wanted to become. I guess I was swept up in the race to the moon. When President Kennedy commissioned the entire nation to be the best you can be. My fascination with flying, my love of heights, and science is what made me want to become an Astronaut. I was very embarrassed the moment when I told my recruiter what I wanted to become. They all laughed out loud as they told each other what I wanted to be. Then he composed himself and told me that I need to grow up, and the best I could be was a mechanic. Math Science and Sports were always my favorite subjects, Physics, Trigonometry, Psychology, and Art I excelled in at Mumford High School in my last years. My last year at school I went to Washington D.C., I visited the NASA research center in the summer. My father was a navigator in the Air Force, that's why I wanted to join. Now I see that being a Negro at the time, there were only a few things that we were able to do. Now that I think about it, it might not been so bad after all to be a mechanic. I went to California to become an actor/ dancer it only took six months till I was on my way back home to join the Detroit Fire Department at my father's request. There were a lot of new things happening in Detroit when I joined the Fire Department. Mayor Coleman A. Young was the first Black Mayor (1972) and he had committed himself to change the Police and Fire Department become fifty percent Black. This action put a lot of racial tension in many Police and Firehouses. White flight was at it's maximum, and there were many vacant homes being set a blaze for fun and profit. 1977 was the year I was assigned to Engine 49, this area became my personal ground to protect, while at work and, later when I got off duty. We received the highest fire service in the city that year. It only took me a few fires to let me know this job was for me. I loved fighting fires, cooking at the fire stations, living, and working in Detroit city streets. I would travel with my equipment everywhere I went if there was a fire I would throw on my equipment and run in to help. This is what I lived for there was no greater feeling than knowing that you are doing what you were created for. I had no idea what hidden plans laid hid for me.

The reason I'm writing this book is to show that in looking for a Career, there will be many obstacles in your way. The only way to find your place in life is to keep searching, keep learning, if someone tells you what you can't do, don't give up. Nothing is going to work out by itself, first you have to first speak it, and then do it, that is how the world was created in the Bible. There will be many obstacles in your way, but if you look hard enough you can find a way around them. If you search hard enough you will find what you search for, another Bible quote, seek and you shall find. I guess my real advice would be to open your mind to accepting a job not exactly what you want but in the field, because through the years you can work toward getting there.

Fire tales are just a part of this book. In this book is the way these incidents really occurred. It is also the way I felt when they happen. Real miracles that happened in these fires which opened my heart back to what I was taught long ago about God. There is a God, I saw his hand as his angels protected my back. The way we learned to fight fires was by telling stories afterwards this would help us in the next fire. My life will be opened up for examination, what I was thinking at the time and what I learned later about certain incidents. I was working on two other manuscripts at the same time, one about relationships, and a Cookbook. I'm putting them all together with my own recipes, and I'm also putting others recipes that firemen taught me. I must thank my love ones that left this earth, my grand parents Walter Haller, Momma O, Conley Abrams SR, and Mother Nora whose love and upbringing gave my parents and I what we needed. My young friends I loved Jesse Bigham who taught me about starting a business, and Garcia Moore a young man with heart who looked up to me as an older brother. To my young nephew Joshua Abrams who was younger but lived longer than I who passed at a very young age. All who lived passing their years searching for a place in this life, as they touched my life. Many times I was to join them, but God saw fit to save me to do another work to show his Grace and Mercy. Last and not the least I thank God for my Mother and Father and how they raised me. Sometimes I feel like I'm the last person raised by a mother and father in the same house. Everyone wasn't blessed the way I was by, having both parents, and a clean up bringing. After finding God again I was told by a Detroit Pastor some good advice, "never let a man stand between you and God". I learned to take it one step further by never letting nothing stand in the way of your goals and dreams.